HALL OF FAITH SERIES

Wings Over New Guinea

The Story of Leonard Barnard

GOLDIE M. DOWN

Pacific Press Publishing Association
Boise, Idaho
Oshawa, Ontario, Canada

Edited by Randy Maxwell
Designed by Consuelo Udave
Cover by Jim Padgett
Type set in 10/12 Century Schoolbook

Copyright © 1988 by
Pacific Press Publishing Association
Printed in United States of America
All Rights Reserved

Library of Congress Catalog Card Number: 88-61120

ISBN 0-8163-0781-4

88 89 90 91 92 • 5 4 3 2 1

Contents

Chapter	1:	The Bombing Raid	5
Chapter	2:	The Reluctant Soldier	11
Chapter	3:	Changing Units	16
Chapter	4:	Wings for Len	25
Chapter	5:	Missionary to the Lepers	32
Chapter	6:	The Leprosarium	39
Chapter	7:	Kai and Kur	45
Chapter	8:	Footslogging in the Mountains	54
Chapter	9:	Wings Over New Guinea	62
Chapter	10:	Prayer and Persistence	70
Chapter	11:	Work for Your Dreams	76

Chapter 1
The Bombing Raid

"I wonder what those planes are doing out at night?"

Standing at the door of the army medical tent, young Len Barnard cocked his head and listened to the distant droning. A moment earlier he had been inside the ward, talking to one of the thirty-six surgical patients under his care. Now, in between listening, he admired the beauty of the tropical evening. A colossal yellow moon balancing on the treetops made the night nearly as bright as day. The cluster of white tents appeared almost luminous, the huge red crosses on their roofs plainly visible in the moonlight.

The hum of aircraft motors became louder, and Len's heart pounded wildly. "They're not Australian planes," he shouted to the patients and their army pals happily crowded into the ward behind him.

The war in the Pacific was still new. There had been no night bombings so far, and no air-raid warning system had been set up. But Len had been in many daytime raids, and he was familiar with the sound of enemy planes. He suspected that these might be Japanese bombers, but he didn't want to alarm his patients until he was sure.

Now another sound separated itself from the engines' drone. A loud *swish, swish, swish* noise arrested his attention and seemed to grow in intensity. Len squinted at the sky. In the brilliant moonlight he saw nothing unusual. Then suddenly he realized what the sound was—falling bombs.

"Down!" he shouted and threw himself to the ground. Behind him in the tent wards he heard scuffling sounds and panicky shouts as men tried to find shelter. There was no time for him to aid the sick and no time for the physically able to race back to their tents and don helmets. There was no time for anyone to rush for the safety of slit trenches—the bombs were on their way.

Whoosh! Bang! The first missile hit a tent only yards away. Len felt the concussion of the blast. Frantically he wriggled into a shallow drain dug to carry off storm water. It was not much protection, but there was nothing else. He grabbed the wooden bottom of a packing case and held it over his head. *Whoosh! Bang! Bang! Bang!* Three more bombs fell in and around the camp.

Bang! Bang! Bang! Len counted seven explosions before the planes finally roared off, and the sound of their motors died in the distance.

"They'll come back," he shouted as he leaped to his feet and rushed into the ward. "Is everyone all right?"

Miraculously everyone was.

"Hurry then." Len rushed from bed to bed, and the other medics helped him lift the helpless patients onto the dirt floor and cover them with the mattresses off their beds.

"Stay there and you'll be all right," Len shouted before joining the others who had dashed outside to collect helmets and crowd into the slit trenches.

As Len ran he saw tents with slashed ropes and shrapnel-shredded canvas leaning drunkenly against each other. Drinking water gushed from tanks pierced by flying fragments, and a flaming incendiary bomb at one end of the encampment bore mute evidence of the raid's success—yet no one had been hurt.

"Thank You, God," Len whispered. All through those terrifyingly long minutes he had called on God to protect them, and He had.

A low humming sound heralded the enemy's second approach. But this time the Australian forces were prepared, and a battery of soldiers on a nearby hillside opened up with anti-aircraft guns. Powerful searchlights probed the sky, and tracer bullets tore through the air like frenzied fireflies.

THE BOMBING RAID 7

Ack-ack-ack-ack! Ack-ack-ack-ack! The night exploded with light and sound as the cowering men in the trenches prayed aloud, calling on God to help them. Len listened in amazement. Tongues that half an hour earlier had uttered blasphemous curses, and lips that had curled in laughter at the latest filthy joke, now pleaded with God for protection.

Len himself prayed. But that was a matter of course. He had always prayed, whether in danger or not. While the groveling men around him begged for safekeeping and promised impossible reformation—to be good, to attend church, to do penance—Len prayed that if it was God's will, they would all be spared.

The noise and terror seemed to climax in a final, fearful thud as a 500-pound bomb hit the ground at the edge of the camp. Len tensed himself and waited for the explosion. None came.

At last it was all over. The drone of plane motors died away in the distance, the anti-aircraft guns fell silent, and even the crackling fire of the incendiary marker-bomb died down.

One by one the soldiers, white-faced and shaken, crawled out of the trenches, and those that were not on duty slunk off to their tents. Len went back to the casualty ward and helped get the patients back to bed and settled for the night.

"You'll be all right now," Len comforted a wide-eyed nineteen-year-old amputee who literally trembled with fear. "It's all over. God saved us. They won't come back tonight."

As soon as the last man was settled, Len and his friend, Laurence, walked around the encampment, inspecting the torn tents, riddled water tanks, and cases of food and medical supplies that sustained damage or were destroyed.

"Just look at that!" Laurence's voice strangled in his throat as he pointed to a dark shape on the ground. Len took a step forward and looked. A bomb, a "daisy cutter" which was intended to explode above ground and cause horrifying destruction, lay half buried in the narrow patch of earth between the two hospital wards.

"If that had gone off—" Len left the sentence unfinished. They both knew what carnage would have resulted if that messenger of death had exploded. More than a hundred men—wounded soldiers and off-duty medics, had been in the nearby wards when the raid began.

"Wow! Look at that thing!" Two of the other men had come up behind to see what Len and Laurence were looking at.

"Cripes, jolly good luck that it didn't have anyone's name on it," the other man laughed coarsely, his promises and prayers of an hour ago already forgotten.

"It was a miracle that it didn't explode," Len exclaimed softly, and under his breath added, "thank You, God. Please continue to watch over me. I want to work for You."

I want to work for You. As far back as anyone could remember, that had been Len Barnard's aim. From infancy Len's godly parents had taught their five children to "love the Lord thy God with all thy heart and thy neighbor as thyself."

While attending church school, Len had decided that he would become a minister and preach God's message to "every nation and kindred and tongue and people." But by the time he reached high school, Len realized that his ambitions would not be easily realized. He had an older brother, two older sisters, and a younger brother—all of whom had to be fed, clothed, and educated too.

These were the sad years of world depression, and a man who had a job of any sort considered himself fortunate. Len's father worked as an engineer in the Sanitarium Health Food Company, and his small wage was always stretched to the limit. There would be no money to pay for a college education.

"I'll have to work for my dream," Len decided. At fourteen, the legal age at which he could leave school, Len began his first job.

The church-affiliated Health Food Company had recently proposed a new scheme to help young people who wanted to continue their education. Len Barnard was the first in New Zealand to take advantage of the program.

"Now you understand, Len," the manager looked at him in fatherly fashion, "you'll work a forty-eight hour week the same as everyone else. Your pay will be ten shillings [one dollar] weekly, and you will be required to pay thruppence [three cents] a week toward your college fees. The company will match every penny that you pay into your college fund. That's a generous offer, m'lad, and I hope you appreciate it."

"Yes, thank you," Len muttered in embarrassed fashion. He knew Brother Blank well as a church member, but this new relationship of employer and employee was something he would have to get used to.

So Len began his working life at the SHF retail shop in Christchurch. It was his job to sweep floors, wipe down shelves and counters, unpack and weigh goods, and wait on customers. Len liked that part most of all. He had been baptized shortly before beginning this job and was still brimming over with the joy of serving Jesus. He smiled as he served the customers. Nothing was too much trouble for him to do; and when he was alone in the back of the store, he sang or whistled as he went about his work.

Of course Len was not a saint. He was just an ordinary boy, and there were days when he didn't sing hymns or whistle—days when he wished he belonged in a wealthy family so he could be out swimming or joy riding with friends instead of slogging away packaging goods in the musty old storeroom or serving in the shop. But Len had been taught to count his blessings, and these woe-is-me feelings did not hit often or last long.

By his seventeenth birthday, Len had enough money to pay his train fare and fees deposit and proceed to Longburn College. He was ecstatic. His dreams were beginning to come true.

Unfortunately, college did not mean the end of work. If anything, Len worked even harder at college than he had at the SHF Company. His pitiful savings melted like a snowball in a volcano. He had not imagined college could be so expensive. Food and lodging and classes to pay for. Textbooks to purchase, soap, toothpaste, offerings, and, occasionally, a pair of socks or some other garment which disappeared in the wash and had to be replaced.

Len was a "D" student, but it had nothing to do with his grades. Being a "D" student meant that he had to work forty hours a week just to keep out of *debt*. At 4:30 every morning, while his more fortunate schoolmates snored comfortably on, Len crawled out of bed to fire the boiler which provided hot water and steam for heating rooms.

As well as work, there were classes to attend. After all, that's why he was at college, to become a minister. Daily class assignments, study periods, and cramming for exams were all necessary parts of that program.

Two years passed swiftly. Busy years but happy ones. Len smiled triumphantly as he clutched his certificate and marched down the wide aisle to receive congratulations along with the rest of his graduating class.

But Longburn was only the first step before attending Avondale, the senior college in Australia. He needed to go there for three or four years to complete his course, but he had no money left. No money to pay his fare by ship across the Tasman Sea. No money for fees or books or clothes or all the other trillion (it seemed) things he would need.

So Len went back to his job at the SHF. It wasn't quite the same as before. He was older and more experienced now. He no longer had to work in the back room. He waited on customers all the time, and another fourteen-year-old, working to earn his college education, swept the floors and wiped the counters and lugged the cartons of foodstuffs around.

Chapter 2
The Reluctant Soldier

In 1939, not long after Len's nineteenth birthday, two things happened which radically changed his life. The first was that the SHF Company asked him to work in Australia and transferred him to their retail store in Brisbane. The second didn't affect him directly at first. For awhile Len wasn't even aware of it, but half a world away, in far-off Europe, a fanatical German with grandiose ideas of world dominion was sowing seeds of war—a war that would last for six years and ultimately affect the lives of millions.

As the months passed and the threat of war became a frightening reality, the leaders of the Seventh-day Adventist Church in Australia and the South Pacific met to consider the problem. As loyal British subjects, they loved their country and were willing to help where they could, but as followers of the Lord Jesus who taught that all men are brothers, they could not condone guns and bombs and killing. Serving in a noncombatant capacity seemed the only way around the problem.

"Conscription is just around the corner, Brethren," one of the leaders warned. "Most of our young men do not want to bear arms. I suggest that we advise them to get some medical training before they are called up. Then they will have no trouble establishing noncombatant status."

Len heeded this advice. Along with some of his friends, he joined one of the many first-aid classes in the city suburbs. The classes were conducted by St. John's Ambulance men, and, to Len's surprise, he found that he really enjoyed this kind of activity. He learned all the resuscitation methods of the day, and also how to cope with shock, treat fractures, and give first-aid for all kinds of emergencies.

Len finished one course and then another and then another. He went on earning certificates until he finally received his bronze medallion and felt qualified to apply for a medical unit when his draft notice came.

One year of war dragged by, and Len received no draft papers. The SHF company dared to hope that his name might have been overlooked, and they transferred him to their Tasmanian branch.

Another year passed before the inevitable happened. His Majesty politely requested the pleasure of Len Barnard's company for three months' compulsory military training.

Len received due recognition of his first-aid certificates and was drafted into a medical unit. He didn't mind that, particularly when some of the other men in the unit told him about a special theater-training assignment at the local hospital. Len applied for this training and, under the auspices of the Australian Army, spent six weeks in Hobart Royal Hospital.

Those six weeks were a high point for young Len Barnard. He spent hours in the operating theater watching the best surgeons and anesthetists at work. He thrilled to the drama of it all. The awe-inspiring precision of a surgeon's hands hurting to heal, the tense struggle to save a life when death hovered near. Len watched amputations, brain surgeries, gall-bladder removals, Caesarean sections, and appendectomies. He marveled at the resilience of the human body. "How can anyone believe in evolution?" he asked himself. "Only God could plan such wonderful bodies as ours."

After his three months' training, Len returned to work, but not for long. By now the Japanese had stormed Pearl Harbor, and the war did not seem so remote at all. Len knew that it was only a matter of time before he would be conscripted into the army, and he rebelled at the thought.

The SHF had transferred Len to their Windsor depot in Victoria by the time he received his orders. Len showed the letter to the manager and then reluctantly presented himself

THE RELUCTANT SOLDIER 13

at the nearest army recruiting station. The interviewing officer studied Len's papers with ill-concealed delight. "We need medics like you," he grunted, and without hesitation assigned Len to a medical unit at Wangaratta.

With a heavy heart, Len lugged his kit into the barracks and looked about him at the bare floors and the rows of double-decker bunks. How would he manage—one Christian among all these worldly-wise young men? It had been bad enough for three months in Tasmania. He endured it then, smug in the knowledge that it was only for a short time. But this was for keeps. Well, as long as the war lasted, anyway.

"Hi there, Soldier. Aren't you Len Barnard?"

Len swung around as a tall, fair-haired young man halted in the doorway, hand outstretched.

"Laurence Gilmore." Len sprang forward and shook the extended hand. "What are you doing here?"

"Same as you. Going to win the war for them." A big grin split Laurence's handsome face.

Len grimaced. "Not willingly, I assure you." He indicated his bunk. "Sit down, Mate, and let's catch up on the news. How long since you were in New Zealand?"

The two Adventists spent the next hour talking. There was so much to say. So much had happened since those far-off days when they had been at Papanui Church School together. Laurence was actually two years younger than Len and in a lower class then. But now, two years made no difference at all, and the friendship renewed that day was to last for life.

Len discovered that Laurence also had done first-aid training in preparation for his military service. Was it coincidence, or was it God's leading that he had been drafted into this same medical unit?

As the days and weeks passed, Len and Laurence grew restless. The training they did in the army unit seemed to be a nonsensical waste of time. What were they accomplishing by sweating in the hot sun, carrying an imaginary stretcher while the sergeant bawled, "Pick up stretcher, one-two! March, three-four!"?

One day an important officer—one of the "big brass"—

visited the camp, and the men were called up for a selection parade. As soon as the preliminaries finished, Colonel Swinbourne addressed the gathering.

"Men, I want to form a medical unit to serve overseas. You know that as conscripts you are here to protect your own country against attack. We cannot ship you out. Only volunteers go overseas."

There was much more to his speech than that, but Len scarcely heard the remainder. As soon as the order came to "Fall out!" he eagerly sought Laurence.

"What about it, Mate? We don't like being in this wretched army, but we can't get out. I'm fed up with this "pick-up-the-stretcher, one-two" business. Why don't we volunteer and get a free trip to wherever? At least we'll see a bit of the world."

Laurence hesitated only a moment. "Good idea, Len," and without a second thought, the two of them marched up to headquarters and volunteered.

Things moved swiftly after that. Within a short time the new unit was formed. The Fifth Casualty Clearing Station, (known as the Fifth CCS) would be sent to Papua New Guinea without delay. The Australian troops there were desperately trying to stem the southward progress of the Japanese invaders and suffering dreadful casualties in the process.

Len and Laurence and the other volunteers traveled by troop train to Sydney, where they were issued overseas gear and granted a few days preembarkation leave.

"That doesn't do us any good," Laurence remarked enviously as the two watched some of their excited companions set off for home and girlfriends. "All of our relatives are in New Zealand."

Len nodded without speaking. He was thinking of a certain young lady who would most definitely be unhappy about his going overseas. He and Mavis had met at college and dated for several years before announcing their engagement. This would mean delaying their plans.

On July 1, 1942, the hospital ship *Wanganella* steamed out of Sydney harbor and headed north with the Fifth CCS on board. They were only a few days out when the ship's radio crackled the news that Japanese minisubmarines had been apprehended sneaking into Sydney harbor by night.

"What do you think of that?" the men asked each other. "At some point we must have passed their mother ship."

The change from Victorian winter to Port Moresby's sweltering heat caught the men by surprise. They had no time to acclimate, and many came down with dengue fever and became the first patients of the Fifth CCS.

Not far away, the battle for Kokoda raged, and Papua New Guinea shuddered under the impact. On both sides men fought and died for their countries. During the short time the Fifth CCS was in nearby Port Moresby, Len counted fifty-seven bombing raids.

It took a little while for the army to get itself organized, and then the Fifth CCS marched seventeen miles north of Port Moresby and set up a casualty clearing station at the edge of the jungle.

Men swarmed around like ants, erecting tents for living quarters and large marquees for wards. They dug slit trenches as a precaution against possible bomb attacks and scraped out shallow channels around each tent to carry off the heavy tropical rain which poured down every afternoon. In practically no time they built two wooden huts to house the operating room, pathology, and medical store.

Despite their hurried efforts, however, wounded men poured in before the encampment was ready for use. Ambulance units brought a constant stream of Kokoda casualties, and Len and Laurence and the other men of the Fifth CCS did their best to rapidly assess their injuries. They gave emergency treatment to those who needed it and sent less urgent cases off to a large general hospital in Port Moresby.

The Fifth CCS medics worked seven days a week in shifts of twelve hours on and twelve hours off. But no one complained. They knew that a few miles farther away their mates were fighting twenty-four hours a day, ceaselessly, week in and week out, trying to stem the invading Japanese forces. Many of them lost limbs, sight, hearing, and even life itself in the desperate battle for freedom.

Chapter 3
Changing Units

Airplanes fascinated Len. During the short time the Fifth CCS spent in Port Moresby, they had been close to the airfield. Len enjoyed hearing the motors roar into life and take off. He learned to recognize the different sounds made by planes in flight: transports and fighters, twin engines and single. He loved to watch the great birds soar up, up, up until they became mere specks in the brilliant blue sky.

Around the perimeter of the airfield a dozen wrecked aircraft looked as if a giant hand had twisted them into frightening, grotesque shapes. Some plane engines were ruined beyond repair, their valves, fuel lines, and electrical wiring fused into one molten mass. Other planes had their wings torn off and undercarriage shattered. A few were pierced and battered but still had their control panels intact. These were the ones that particularly caught Len's attention.

As often as he could he sneaked over to the airfield and wandered in and out among the wrecked aircraft, examining crumpled aluminum and tangled wiring. Running his hand caressingly over torn wings, fingering pump and propeller. If he found an accessible cockpit, he'd worm his way into the pilot's seat and, studying the now useless instruments and controls, he'd wriggle the joy stick and pretend he was flying.

Each time he made one of these excursions into the magical world of flying, Len returned to camp with strengthened resolve to become a pilot. Yes, he was positive that by God's grace he'd be a pilot and fly one of those wonderful machines.

Not to carry death and destruction, however. Oh no. He would fly his airplane on missions of mercy.

Missions of mercy. Len liked the sound of that phrase. He wasn't sure whether he'd originated it or whether he'd read it somewhere, but it sounded grand when he told Laurence about his determination to fly.

"Great idea," Laurence congratulated him as they talked together after one of their prayer sessions. "I'm sure the Lord will find work for us to do—if the war ever ends and we get out of this miserable army."

Both young men preferred night duties. That way they could sleep mornings and have afternoons free. Prayer was almost impossible in their crowded tent-barracks, so they would hike across to one of the hills surrounding the camp on three sides and have their prayer sessions there. A certain tree with low leafy branches formed a natural "private place," and in this green cathedral they talked to God and to each other.

They were young and full of dreams and plans for the future—if there was to be any future. Their daily contact with the terrible sights and sounds of war, and their enforced association with many godless fellow soldiers, made them wonder how God put up with the wickedness of humankind.

Sabbaths brought a welcome relief. Len and Laurence often managed to get the day off and thumb a ride to Port Moresby or wherever they knew fellow believers were gathered.

"Funny, isn't it?" Len remarked to Laurence. "Adventists are attracted to each other like iron filings to a magnet. That Rod Fowler in ANGAU keeps his eyes out for all of us young fellows. Did you know him before you came to Papua New Guinea?"

"No. He was up here working with a government medical department before the war began. When the army came in and took charge, the Australia New Guinea Administrative Unit became a branch of the army, caring for the native population. That's why it's called ANGAU, you know."

"Yes, I know. I think Rod's life is more interesting than ours."

18 WINGS OVER NEW GUINEA

Army life was not exactly a bed of roses for either young man. Even though they were in a noncombatant unit, religious prejudice reared its ugly head. Not so much among their fellow soldiers, but the colonel in command belonged to a totally different denomination, and he made it hard for the two Seventh-day Adventists in his unit.

"We need medics like you in ANGAU," Rod Fowler said when he heard of the troubles Len and Laurence were having in camp. "Why don't you ask for a transfer?"

"Ask for a transfer?" Len mocked good-naturedly. "We'd have as much hope of transferring to the moon. The colonel is very possessive of his Fifth CCS, and he wouldn't part with any of us. I'd dearly love to work with ANGAU, but there isn't a chance."

"At least put in your application," Rod urged. "We'll all pray about it. If God wants you in ANGAU, He will work a miracle."

Encouraged by Rod's faith, both boys applied for a transfer to ANGAU. At first this appeared to be the worst thing they could have done. The colonel apparently took it as a personal insult that anyone should want to leave his unit, and his anger could not be appeased. If things had been unpleasant before, they now became intolerable.

All the other doctor-officers and staff knew what conscientious workers Len and Laurence were, but no matter what they did or how meticulously they did it, it was still wrong as far as the colonel was concerned. He found fault on the slightest provocation and regularly assigned them to the worst jobs in the camp.

He sent Laurence to dig latrine pits. Digging holes fifteen feet deep through rock and clay is not easy work under any circumstances, and digging under a broiling tropical sun is almost unbearable. But Laurence did it.

Things came to a head one day when the colonel ordered Len to do something in the ward.

"Yes, Sir," Len replied. But as he was in the middle of carrying out a complicated surgical dressing on a seriously wounded soldier, he completed that task before attending to the colonel's assignment.

The colonel was furious. "Insubordination," he roared. "I'll have you arrested for failing to obey a reasonable order."

In the army no one answers back or tries to explain his conduct to a commanding officer, so Len had no chance to justify his short delay. Instead, after a brief court-martial, he had to silently submit when two hefty MPs (military policemen) marched him off to an army prison unit.

Demotion was automatic. The stripes were ripped off Len's uniform, and he was issued with prison garb, given a sledge hammer, and set to work breaking rocks. It all happened so quickly that Len scarcely had time to collect his thoughts.

When he did have a chance to reflect, Len felt so delighted to be out of the stressful atmosphere of the hospital and away from the petty persecution of the colonel, that he attacked the rocks with great gusto.

"What on earth are you doing here?" One of the prison officers who had once been a patient, walked by.

"Cracking rocks," Len grinned happily

"I can see that. I mean, what did you do that made them put you in the clink?"

"Find out for yourself." Len attacked the rocks as if they were the colonel himself.

The officer shook his head. "There's something wrong somewhere. Don't worry. I'll get you out of here and back to the hospital, soldier."

"No way." Len's grin widened. "I got out of there only an hour ago. I'd rather break stones than go back."

Despite his brave words Len felt humiliated. Being sentenced to camp prison was the worst thing that could happen to a soldier. Not only did it put a stigma against his name, but he lost both rank and pay.

"Bother that colonel!" Len brought his hammer down so hard on the next rock that a sharp chip flew off it and hit him on the shin.

"Ouch!" Len yelled with pain. Blood streamed down his leg, and a guard came running and led him off to the prison first-aid tent.

"Hey," the young medic said when he examined Len's gash,

"that needs stitches, Man. I'd better take you across to the Fifth CCS hospital."

"No way," Len shook his head. "It'll be all right without stitches. Clean the blood off and pull the edges together with tape, like this." He showed the first-aider what to do. "I've treated dozens of wounds worse than this. It'll be all right."

"Well, you can't go back to work," the medic insisted. "I'll assign you to help one of the camp officers for a couple of weeks."

The official to whom Len was assigned happened to be his former patient. He smiled when Len presented himself for light duties, "I told you I'd get you off breaking rocks," he reminded.

"You had nothing whatever to do with it," Len retorted. "I did it myself."

"Oh well," the officer winked, "how about tidying up the recreation tent? Guess that'll take you a couple of weeks."

"Thanks a lot," Len said happily, and spent his two weeks' prison sentence doing nothing more arduous than sitting in a camp chair chewing gum and reading books. Best of all, as Len later recognized, his imprisonment was part of the answer to his prayers. A short time after his release he was transferred to the medical division of ANGAU.

"You see, Dear," Len wrote to his beloved Mavis, "no commanding officer can refuse to transfer a soldier from one unit to another if the transfer means promotion for that man. Being imprisoned automatically canceled my rank, so a transfer to ANGAU was a promotion, and the colonel legally had to let me go. How wonderfully God works out His will."

(Not long afterwards God worked a miracle for Laurence, and he, too, was transferred to ANGAU. The friends worked together for a short time, but eventually they were sent to different areas. After the war, in God's providence, Laurence and his wife, June, became medical missionaries.)

Len had scarcely dumped his kit in his new barracks when he was hustled off to Port Moresby Hospital to do a three-month course in tropical medicine. And what a course it proved to be. The doctors were dedicated, experienced men, thorough in their methods and eager to help the students learn. Tropical medicine was an entirely new area for Len, and he studied hard.

Shortly after Len finished this training period, the commanding officer of ANGAU sent him out to take charge of a field hospital situated close to three labor camps where nationals were employed. Now Len was in his element. While he pitied their ignorance and consequent illnesses and accidents, Len loved the simple native people, many of them as yet untouched by the white man's civilization.

He liked his small bush hospital too. Set in the middle of a cleared space on a verdant hillside, Len could stand outside the main door and look at the towering, cloud-capped mountains stretching far into the distance. Here and there, ugly brown patches scarred the jungle-covered slopes, and Len knew that these marked the sites of primitive villages, accessible only by plodding for days up narrow, tortuous trails.

"Someday I'll visit them," he promised himself. "Someday they will all receive medical treatment and hear the gospel message. Someday I'll fly like a bird over those mountaintops."

One afternoon, Len received a note from a senior officer at a nearby military camp. "Please check these fifty cargo-boys for me. They've just arrived after a long and difficult trek."

Len knew what "cargo-boys" meant. Not many of the indigenous people had been trained to bear arms, but they did what they could to assist the Australian and American forces who unitedly defended their country. Hundreds of them served as ambulance bearers, and hundreds more acted as porters, carrying heavy loads on head or back over trails that white men considered impossible.

The "Fuzzy Wuzzies," as the Allies dubbed the Papua New Guineans because of their frizzy black hair, were accustomed to arduous journeys by foot over almost inaccessible mountains and through dense, impenetrable jungles. The war might not have ended as it did without their help.

When the fifty carriers stumbled down the track and lined up in front of his outpost hospital, Len gasped. He'd never seen such a pitiful group of natives. They were thin to the point of emaciation and suffering from malnutrition. Most had been stricken with a variety of tropical diseases as well, and he ordered them straight into hospital.

But the condition of the last six men puzzled Len. They were just as thin and malnourished as the others, but their skin was not dirty and scaly. They did not have any illnesses, and they seemed to be happier. They even managed weak, grateful smiles as he examined them.

"Which way you walkabout one time other fella man all together time?" he asked in pidgin English. [Did you walk all the way with the other men?]

"Yes, Sir." They nodded their frizzy heads emphatically.

"You fella kai kai all the same other fella men?" [Have you eaten the same food as the other men?]

"Yes." They nodded.

Then Len asked whether they had been medical orderlies at any time and carried medicine for themselves.

"No got." All six shook their heads in swift denial.

Len's puzzlement increased. There was absolutely no doubt that these men were different from the other forty-four. But in what way? He had to find out. Suddenly he had an idea. "You fella Christian?" he asked.

"Yes," they chorused. They were Christian Mission boys. Not only that, they were Seventh-day Adventist Mission boys.

"Me too. Me fella Seven-day." Len pointed to himself.

Now the Fuzzy Wuzzie smiles stretched ear to ear. Beaming with happiness, the six crowded around Len to shake his hand. In pidgin they told him that he was the first white Seventh-day Adventist they had seen for more than a year. Because of enemy advances, their own missionaries had been forced to leave the isolated area where they lived.

When work ended for the day, the six cargo boys came around to Len's quarters for worship and talk. Little by little Len pieced their story together.

These six men were not mountain boys. They were coastal natives whom the missionaries had taken with them to help open up mission work in the high mountain villages. But they had only been working a few months when the war began and the government ordered all foreigners to leave Papua New Guinea.

The missionaries' departure left the six coastal men alone among savages who were capable of every kind of witchcraft and treachery, and who fought constantly with the people in the adjoining villages. Despite all this, the six determined to be true to God and to do what they could to teach the gospel to their countrymen.

Some time later, the enemy soldiers in this mountain area drew back a little, and the Australian Army decided to try to cut a track from this savage hinterland to the coast. A couple of army officers were dropped into the area, and they selected fifty men—including the six Christians—to act as porters and help them blaze a trail to the south.

Their planned route led through cannibal country, and more than once the party was ambushed and viciously attacked. The officers resorted to guns and fought their way out. Day and night the lives of leaders and carriers were in danger, and in order to stay alive they had to forgo rest and sleep and keep moving. In many places dense bush and tangled vines impeded their progress, and they had to hack their way through the jungle.

Finally, the cannibal country and seemingly never-ending mountains lay behind, but there was no shortage of other troubles. Crocodile-infested marshes, deadly snakes, leeches, and poisonous thorns, besides myriads of malarial mosquitoes, flooded streams, sharp rocks, and slippery mud. Then, as if this wasn't enough, they ran out of supplies.

For two weeks the carriers plodded on, weary and faint for lack of food. Many of them ate leaves, but that only made them sick. Then one afternoon the leading carriers seemed to suddenly go berserk. They dropped their loads and ran shouting into the bush.

"Pig! Pig!" Like lighting the word passed back along the line. The men had seen and were chasing a wild pig. The carriers took advantage of the unscheduled stop and set down their gear and waited for the others to return. In a short time they came crashing triumphantly through the undergrowth with a dead wild pig trussed to a hastily cut pole.

As soon as they made camp that night, the carriers built a fire and roasted the pig. Too hungry to wait until it was properly cooked, they dragged the animal from the burning coals and tore it apart, handing a small portion to each starving man.

Only the six Seventh-day Adventists refused to eat. In vain the Australian officers tried to persuade them to take some of the pork. "Aren't you hungry?" he demanded.

Yes, they were just as hungry as the other men, but the missionaries had taught them that their bodies belonged to God, and He did not want them to eat unclean foods. No amount of argument or abuse could make them compromise their conscience.

Conditions worsened daily. One of the carriers became too sick to walk, and the patrol officers did not know what to do with him. Then the six Christians offered to carry him. In their weakness, they struggled to carry the crude bush stretcher with its miserable load added to their burden. Every hour or so they stepped aside into the bush beside the trail and prayed, asking God to give them strength to keep going.

At last the jungle thinned, and even the sickest and weakest in the party managed a cry of joy as they staggered toward a riverside village. The villagers gave them food and provided canoes to float the whole party downstream to the coast. After three months of incredible hardship the nightmare journey was over.

"Me fella tank God." The spokesman for the six finished his story and looked reverently heavenward.

"Yes indeed, thank God for keeping you all safe." Len's eyes brimmed with tears, and he shook hands all around again. In his heart, ambition had kindled anew. He knew what he wanted to do with his life. As soon as the war ended he wanted to be a medical missionary—a medical missionary who would fly on missions of mercy to help people such as these.

Chapter 4
Wings for Len

After Len completed seventeen months' service in Papua New Guinea, the army granted him a home leave. Officially his leave was only forty-five days, but because his folks lived in New Zealand, and the war made transport between the two countries extremely irregular, he received an additional forty-five days.

Three months away from the hell of war, hatred, and death. Plenty of time for Len and Mavis to be married and enjoy some time together before Len returned to his ANGAU hospital and would once again have nothing to link his love to his bride except prayer and the postal service.

During this next period in an ANGAU hospital, Len met a young Seventh-day Adventist teacher named Mamatau. When the government ordered the overseas missionaries to leave Papua New Guinea, Mamatau was left to carry on work in a certain village.

Although he felt lonely in this strange village, far away from his own tribe, Mamatau faithfully did his best. Morning and evening he called the villagers together for worship, and during the day he taught school for the children and any adults who wanted to attend. On Sabbaths he conducted Sabbath School and church service in the small, native-built church. Everyone in the village attended Mamatau's meetings, and many of them, although not yet baptized, tried to serve the Lord.

A unit of the Japanese Army stationed nearby somehow

heard of Mamatau's activities. They became suspicious because he taught some of his classes in English. They sent for him and accused him of spying for the Australians.

"No," Mamatau denied the charge. "I am not working for Australians. I am working for God."

But the officer who conducted the interrogation did not believe Mamatau and angrily commanded him to stop teaching the people to speak English. "We are winning the war," he shouted. "The Australians won't be coming back. You don't need to speak their language."

"Sir, I teach English so that the people can read the Bible for themselves," protested Mamatau.

But the angry officer would not listen. "No more!" he shouted and waved Mamatau away.

Mamatau trudged slowly back to his village. The missionary had left him in charge and expected him to conduct school in the usual manner—English and all. But now the enemy had told him not to teach, and if he did he would be in trouble. What should he do?

As Mamatau walked he prayed, and suddenly a text sprang into his mind, "We ought to obey God rather than man." Yes, that was his answer. He would do as God wanted him to do, and God would look after him.

A few weeks later, some enemy soldiers appeared at the door of the large grass hut where Mamatau was teaching school. They looked very fierce and demanded that Mamatau and two of his friends accompany them to the commanding officer.

"Didn't I tell you not to teach English to those villagers?" demanded the officer. "You are defying me. Now, once more I command you, do not teach the people to speak English. Do not teach them Christianity. We allow only one type of worship in this country—worship of the emperor of Japan."

With a prayer in his heart, Mamatau respectfully replied that he could not refrain from preaching about Christ and teaching the people to read the Bible.

In great rage the officer leaped to his feet and brandished his sword at Mamatau and shouted: "You obey me or I cut off your head!"

WINGS FOR LEN 27

Mamatau and his friends walked slowly back to their jungle village, discussing the threat and wondering what he should do. The missionaries had urged Mamatau to preach the gospel to the heathen. But if the enemy killed him, there would be nobody to teach school and preach. Then the people would have no chance of learning the gospel. Would it be better to obey the order and just teach and preach in secret?

Stepping off the trail, Mamatau and the two men knelt down in the jungle and asked God to show them what they should do. When they finished praying, they all agreed that they would go ahead with their work. God's Word said: "Go ye into all the world and preach the gospel," and that's what they were doing. If they were obedient, God would do His part.

Two Sabbaths later the villagers gathered into the small leaf thatched church, and, with the aid of a tattered but precious picture roll, Mamatau conducted Sabbath School. Afterward they sang some hymns, and Mamatau began the church service.

Suddenly a band of shouting soldiers surrounded the church, and an officer with fixed bayonet charged inside. He looked around among the terrified villagers until he saw Mamatau. Yelling abuse at the teacher, he grabbed his arm and began to drag him outside.

Although frightened, Mamatau remained calm. "Please let me finish the service," he said to his captor. "The people are innocent. They have only come to hear me preach. You have surrounded the church with your soldiers, and I cannot get away."

The man saw the sense of that reasoning and reluctantly gave permission for Mamatau to continue speaking. The soldiers outside crowded into the doorway and listened as Mamatau pleaded with the village people to be faithful to God even if it meant losing their lives. He prayed for them, and they sang a hymn together. Then with tears in their eyes they all said goodbye to Mamatau, believing that it would be the last time they would see him and his two young converts.

The congregation filed sadly out of church, and the soldiers let them go. Then Mamatau and the two youths walked toward the waiting officer.

"Didn't I tell you that I would kill you if you preached Christianity again?" The officer threateningly raised his sword.

"Yes sir. We are ready to die now." Mamatau and his two friends closed their eyes in prayer and waited quietly for the blow to fall.

But it didn't. After waiting a few moments, they opened their eyes and saw that the officer had replaced his sword and he and his soldiers were conversing in Japanese.

The officer beckoned to Mamatau and told him that he and his men admired the courage with which he served his God. "We can see that you love your God and serve him as loyally as we serve our emperor," he said. "If you will promise not to send messages to the Australian Army, we will allow you to continue your work."

"Of course we promised," Mamatau smilingly assured Len as he finished telling his story. "We kept our word and they kept theirs and we had no more trouble from the enemy."

"How wonderfully God protects those who love and serve Him," Len replied thoughtfully. His ambition to become a missionary had received another boost.

When the war ended, the soldiers working with ANGAU were required to serve an additional six months until the government could reorganize and take over the civilian medical work. No one was happy about this, least of all Len, who was impatient to get home to his wife and the infant daughter he had never seen.

During this time, however, he often met Seventh-day Adventist missionaries who were returning to their posts. They eased his loneliness and brought him news of home and church. As they visited together, Len told the missionaries of his burning desire to serve the Lord.

"We need fellows like you," they replied. "There's plenty of work to do."

"But I haven't been to college," Len demurred. "I couldn't preach or teach."

"Nonsense." They waived his objections aside. "We can do

the preaching and the teaching. We need fellows like you to do the medical work—open up clinics, start a leper colony. Why don't you apply for mission work? Tell the union conference what you can do."

"All right," Len agreed, and quickly sent off a letter.

Weeks seemed like years as Len waited for the mail to bring an answer to his application. "Oh, God, if it be Thy will, open the way for me to be a missionary," he prayed as he waited.

At last the reply came. Len's hands trembled as he slit open the envelope. His eyes raced across the typed words.

"Dear Brother Barnard," the writer said, "we appreciate your willingness to serve the Lord in the mission field, but at present there is no vacancy in the organized work."

For long minutes Len sat stunned with disappointment. Then slowly his disjointed thoughts came together. He had prayed for the Lord's will to be done, and this was the answer. Apparently God didn't need him in the mission field. All right then, what would he do with his life?

A cool breeze rattled the shutters as Len sat, chin in hand, at the rickety table he called his desk. A crow in a tree nearby uttered its raucous "Caw, caw." Len didn't notice it. Submerged in despondency, he couldn't see beyond his disappointment. Presently, familiar words, like pieces of a jigsaw, formed in his mind. What was that quotation now, something about "God never closes one door but that He opens another"?

Len turned the words over and over in his mind. Was that it? Did the Lord want him to take medical training, to be a doctor and not a missionary? All the doctor friends he had made during his service in New Guinea had urged him to take medical training.

"You're a natural, Len," they said. "Why don't you go to medical school and qualify? We'll guarantee that you get through." A wink and a nod accompanied this promise, and Len felt sure that they really would help him if he needed it.

As soon as he was demobilized from the army Len hurried back to New Zealand. After a few wonderful weeks at home with Mavis and baby Sharyn, he applied for government education aid for returned soldiers. This was granted and the family moved to Australia, where he enrolled in the university. But it did not take long for Len to realize that he was not equal to the task. A strange restlessness possessed him. More than a decade had slipped by since he finished school, and he could not settle down to study. The responsibility of caring for a wife and baby did not help either.

After four years of war and privation in New Guinea, it felt great to be back in civilization again, and Len was eager to get on with his life—to succeed in something. But no matter how hard he tried, he just could not settle down to the grueling medical studies.

For weeks Len and Mavis worried and prayed about the problem. What should he do? What did the Lord want him to do? They received no clear direction from any quarter, and at last, in desperation Len decided to go back and work in ANGAU.

"I've got to do something, Mavis." Len paced up and down their tiny living room. "I've got to earn some money. We can't exist on love and fresh air. Not with the baby and all." He paused to stroke baby Sharyn's downy head. "I'll get in touch with Rod Fowler; he's still in New Guinea. You and the baby will come with me, of course. The war's over now and the government's in charge. There'll be plenty of other mothers and children up there."

As Len expected, he had no trouble at all getting back with ANGAU, only it wasn't called ANGAU anymore. It was now under civilian control and had become the Government Medical Department of Papua New Guinea.

"A rose by any other name would smell as sweet," Len quoted to Mavis. "It will be the same kind of work but under better conditions."

"Well, you'll be happy." Mavis smiled fondly at him. "You wanted to be a medical missionary, and this is the next best thing."

"Yes." Len nodded. "But I'll tell you one thing, my Dear, I'm not going back there until I learn to fly. It's a costly business, but I've got some accumulated pay to collect from the army, and I'm going to spend it on flying lessons."

"So you can fly on missions of mercy?" Mavis teased.

Mavis may not have been keen on Len's learning to fly, but she knew that it was useless to protest. Len loved her and his baby daughter, she was sure of that. But sometimes she wondered whether he wasn't even more in love with his dream of flying.

True to his promise, toward the close of 1946, Len enrolled in flying lessons. Every day at the airfield he thrilled as he watched the big metal birds emerge from their hangars, taxi down the runway, and gracefully take off into the clouds.

"I'll be doing that soon," he promised himself.

Len's instructor was a veteran pilot of the first world war, and his teaching lacked nothing. Len pored over dials and diagrams. He learned the laws of aerodynamics and the precise skills of navigation. He became well acquainted with the workings of the motor and what made it tick. He memorized air-safety rules and emergency procedures and learned to respect the subtleties of the weather. There was so much more to this flying business than he had expected.

Then one day, almost breathless with excitement, Len donned flying helmet and goggles, and he and his instructor climbed into a plane and took to the skies. Strapped into the open cockpit of the small, two-winged Tiger Moth, with hurricane-force wind whistling past his ears, Len was overcome with a feeling of exhilaration. For years he had dreamed of this day, and back in New Guinea he had prepared himself for it as he studied the instrument panels and jiggled the joy sticks of crashed aircraft.

"Just don't become too confident," the instructor warned as they clambered out of the plane afterward. "Flying is inherently safe but very unforgiving. Learn it well."

Within a relatively short time, Len completed his course and earned his license. Now he was a pilot. A pilot without a plane, however, with precious little hope of ever having one.

"Never mind about that," Len told himself optimistically. "I'm like the great statesman who said: 'I shall prepare myself, and someday my chance will come.' I've done my part, I have prepared, and someday my chance will come."

Chapter 5
Missionary to the Lepers

Len's first position after joining the struggling public health department of Papua New Guinea was administrator of a hospital in Bogia, ninety miles along the coast from Madang.

"You'll find a lot of lepers in that district," the superintendent at Madang told Len. "If you want to treat them, you have my permission. But first you'd better come along to the hospital and learn a bit more about the disease."

To date, Len's knowledge of leprosy had been almost nil. In ANGAU he had treated local people, but they were war casualties or accident victims or an occasional urgent medical case. There had been no time for continual treatments, and no beds available for long-term illnesses; and certainly there was no separate building where lepers could be isolated from the other patients.

The Barnards spent a few months at headquarters while Len learned all he could about treating leprosy and amputating affected limbs. At Bogia he would be in sole charge of the hospital. There would be no higher authority to whom he could turn for advice. This thought troubled Len, and he followed the doctor around like a shadow—watching, asking, doing, trying to store up every particle of information that might prove useful.

The three months in Madang gave Mavis time to adapt to life in Papua New Guinea. In New Zealand Len had talked for hours about what to expect, but nothing he said prepared her for the reality—the homesickness, the enervating heat, the lack of amenities, and the dreadful aftermath of war.

She had so many new things to learn—how to bake bread—there was no corner bakery to which she could turn, how to cook without gas and iron without electricity, how to train someone to help her in the house, and how to be patient when that "someone" smashed the crockery and wiped her flat, brown nose with the dish towel, how to do without packaged cereals and canned goods, and how to use coconuts and yams and papaya and many other strange foods in their place. It was a time of adjustment for both of them, and they needed to learn all they could before they were left to manage on their own.

At his new hospital, Len found it just as the doctor had predicted. There were the usual malarial patients and fevers and spear wounds and broken bones, but the leprosy patients outnumbered all the rest.

As soon as word spread that a new "doctor" had arrived and that now that the war was over he would be able to treat leprosy, the unfortunate sufferers flocked to the hospital. Len and his medical orderlies worked like machines, cleaning and bandaging ulcers, giving injections, and distributing medicines and tablets.

The plight of the lepers wrung Len's heart. Many of them were advanced cases. Many had no fingers or toes. In most cases leprosy destroys nerves, and the infected person loses his sense of pain. He may scratch his hand or leg on a poisonous thorn or stub his toe on a sharp rock, and because he cannot feel anything, the injury is not treated and becomes infected, the infection eats away his flesh, and he loses fingers, toes, nose, lips, or ears. Len saw some dreadful sights.

"The earlier leprosy is recognized, the easier it is to treat," Len explained to Mavis. "Lepers are never cured. The disease may be arrested, but a leper can never consider himself free from the threat of recurrence. A lot of these dreadful disfigurements could be prevented if they were treated early enough," Len mourned to Mavis. "Oh, if only we could go out into the villages and find the lepers in the early stages of the disease." He looked longingly at the sky, and Mavis knew he was dreaming his impossible dream of a flying medical service in Papua New Guinea.

"I worry that you may bring some of the germs home to Sharyn," Mavis said nervously. "I know it isn't common for white people to get leprosy, but it's not impossible, is it?"

"No, it's not impossible." Len smiled fondly at her. "But leprosy is not as contagious as a common cold, my Love. I take all precautions, and I'm quite sure that you and Sharyn will not catch any 'germs.'"

A year flew swiftly by, and Len and Mavis began to think of long-range plans. In another six months their term of service would end, and what would they do then? Should Len sign on for another term, or would they go home and try to find congenial work in New Zealand?

They talked the problem over from every angle and prayed about it. Len could not forget the hours during war service when he and Laurence had prayed under a tree and how they had dedicated their lives to God for service. Surely God would accept their gift.

One afternoon an unexpected visitor flew in to Bogia. Pastor Robert Frame, the president of the Seventh-day Adventist mission in Papua New Guinea had come from Port Moresby especially to see them.

"Brother Barnard," he said, "we need you to begin a leper colony up in the highlands. The government is planning to build a hospital and equip it, and they are asking us to operate it. We have quite a few medical missionaries in Papua New Guinea, but you are the only man with the specialized expertise that is necessary. I have come to ask you to apply to the union conference for mission service."

Len's face broke into one huge, beaming smile. "I did that more than two years ago," he said. "I don't need to apply again."

Three hours later the president flew back to Port Moresby, leaving behind a dazed but happy couple.

"I can't believe it's true." Len sank back in a wicker chair on their screened-in veranda and gazed across at Mavis and Sharyn sharing another wicker chair. "We're going to be missionaries, Mavis. Real live missionaries and work for the Lord."

As soon as Len's twenty-one month contract with the government ended, the Barnards took a short leave in New Zealand and then returned to Papua New Guinea to begin their mission service. But not even Len, with six years in Papua New Guinea behind him, was prepared for what being a missionary really meant.

On a pleasantly warm June day in 1949, the three Barnards left the sunny climate and comparative comfort of Port Moresby, and flew into the highlands in a tiny 'stick and cloth' Dragon biplane.

The difference struck them forcibly as they stared down at the jungle below them. No sign of roads; no bridges across streams. Here and there a brown patch in the sea of green trees betrayed the presence of a native village, but there were no tin-roofed houses anywhere.

High, tree-capped mountains dwarfed the tiny plane, and, lacking the altitude to fly above them, the pilot skillfully maneuvered the small craft between the rugged mountaintops.

"Where will we land?" Mavis whispered to Len. "There don't seem to be any flat places at all down there."

"Oh, there must be an airstrip somewhere," Len said airily, but all the same he peered anxiously out of the tiny window.

Finally, spread out below like a pocket handkerchief, the airstrip appeared.

"Fasten you seat belts and extinguish your cigarettes," the pilot quipped light-heartedly. "Hang on, now. We're going in."

The local government officer greeted them cheerily as they climbed stiffly out of the ancient plane and shivered in the bleak highland atmosphere at Mount Hagan.

"Yep, bit colder up here, eh?" The officer bundled their suitcases and boxes of belongings into a battered army jeep. "Climb in," he invited, "and we'll be on our way."

Climb in? Len couldn't see anywhere left for them to climb into, but he pushed boxes and bundles aside so that Mavis could perch on a tiny space of seat and hold Sharyn in her arms, while he balanced precariously on a pile of bedding.

"She's a bit bumpy," the government officer observed nonchalantly as they bounced and lurched over the primitive road. "It's always like this after rain."

"But I thought it rained every day up here," Mavis whispered to Len who grinned encouragingly. "Cheer up. The road doesn't go far."

The words were scarcely out of his mouth when the jeep jerked to a stop, and a group of wild-looking men appeared as if emerging out of the ground.

"The porters will take your stuff," the officer explained, "and Wagie here," he indicated a burly New Guinean with a bone through his nose, "will carry the little girl."

Fortunately, three-year-old Sharyn had not forgotten her little brown playmates at Bogia and Madang, and she fearlessly rode on Wagie's broad shoulders.

For seven torturous miles the party plodded uphill, gasping for breath in the rarefied 7,000-foot altitude and slipping and sliding on the oozing mud trail. Three weary hours later they scaled the last ridge and viewed the site of the future leper colony, six hundred acres of land covered with tall swamp reeds that the natives called *pit-pit*.

Len stood enthralled, gloating over the wide expanse. Already he saw it cleared and organized in streets with rows of clean, neat huts surrounded by luxuriant gardens, and peopled with happy, successfully treated lepers.

"Where are we going to live?" Mavis's plaintive question shattered Len's prophetic dream and jolted him back to the present.

"Eh? Oh, I guess they have something for us. Temporarily," he added when he saw the expression on Mavis's face, "until we can build a decent house."

They did. The cheery government official led them to a large, grass-roofed hut with plaited bamboo floor and ceiling.

"I'm sorry we can't offer you better accommodation." He became uncomfortably aware of Mavis's brimming eyes. "But it's only temporary," he echoed Len's assurances.

"Only temporary! It will take ages and ages to fell trees and

MISSIONARY TO THE LEPERS 37

saw wood and build a decent house." Mavis managed a watery smile. She wiped her eyes in an obvious attempt to make the best of it, but she refused to enter the hut until one of the men went in and assured her that there were no frogs, rats, or snakes inside.

Six weeks later, when the Barnards had settled in as best they could, five officials from the Coral Sea Union Mission visited them to talk over plans for the leper colony. A cold wind blew through the hut's grass walls, and rain dripped mournfully from the sodden leaf roof. After supper the group crouched around a blazing fire in the center of what served as the living room. Before retiring, Len doused the fire with a jug of water, and soon both family and visitors were sound asleep.

About an hour later Len awoke to an unusual crackling sound. Wearily he opened his eyes and saw a strange red glow in the woven ceiling. It took only a split second for him to realize what it meant. "Fire!" he yelled and dashed into the big room to wake the other men.

Faster than it takes to tell, the entire ceiling and then the walls burst into flames. Billowing smoke choked the men as they snatched whatever they could reach and raced outside. Len stumbled back to the bedroom where Mavis stood dazed and immobilized with fright. He grabbed Sharyn from her cot, seized Mavis's hand, and the three of them reached safety with not a moment to spare.

In less then two minutes it was all over. The shocked and shivering group watched the flames die down into glowing embers. Everything that the Barnards possessed had vanished in fire and smoke.

"Some of the hot ash must have flown up into the ceiling when you doused the fire, Len," the president speculated. "I suppose it took an hour or so to smolder into flame. It's lucky we weren't all roasted in our sleep."

"God certainly had His hand over us," Len said humbly, and the rest murmured husky amens.

Local inhabitants offered the refugees shelter for the remainder of the night, at the same time making it clear that such calamities were only to be expected when white people disregarded the power of Kur—the spirit god of the Togobans. Only then did the missionaries learn that the government had built the Barnards' hut on a former "sing-sing" site—an area the natives used for scared dances to Kur.

"Pure coincidence, of course," the missionaries agreed, but it would be hard to convince the local people of that.

When daylight came, the bedraggled survivors slipped and slithered down the dangerous trail, seven miles back to Mount Hagan; from there they flew out to the coast.

Sympathetic friends helped them recuperate emotionally, and six weeks later the Barnards were back at Togoba, with considerably fewer belongings than before, but with another mission couple, carpenter Frank Aveling and his wife, Ida, to help build the leper colony.

The first thing that had to be done was to clear the land and plant gardens. The next thing was to build huts for the lepers to live in and a temporary hospital where they could be treated.

Len and Frank and their native helpers worked from sunup to sundown, lacking almost every facility. As far as possible they built in native fashion and used native materials. Every piece of timber used for framework had to be cut by hand and pit-sawn into planks. Every nail and screw, every hammer and saw, every sheet of roofing iron and length of drainpipe, had to be flown in from port cities, which made costs soar.

Mavis and Ida Aveling battled along as best they could without any of the amenities that were accepted as necessities at home. They had no running water, gas, electricity—or shops if they happened to run out of any food items. They had no fresh vegetables or fruit until the garden began to produce, no postal service, no telephone, no newspaper, no doctor or dentist, no friends to visit, no—the list was endless.

"It's a good thing that we're always so busy," Mavis wrote to her mother. "I don't have time to miss all the things we haven't got. We have each other and we have Sharyn, and we are in the place that God wants us to be and doing the work that God wants us to do. That's all that really matters."

Chapter 6
The Leprosarium

Within nine months of the Barnards' arrival, the leprosarium opened its doors for patients. True, most of the buildings were simple grass-roofed huts, and the garden had scarcely reached top productivity, but Len decided they couldn't wait any longer. "There are so many things yet to be done that it will take years of hard work to get it finished. We'll begin now and grow as we go."

News of the hospital's opening quickly spread through the jungle villages, and more and more lepers came for treatment. Len was soon overwhelmed with the work, and his desperate pleas for help brought two nurses from Australia, Olive and Elsie Pearce.

Their arrival delighted Mavis even more than it did Len. The Avelings had moved on, and she missed Ida. Olive and Elsie gallantly lightened Len's workload, and also provided female company which helped relieve Mavis's loneliness.

Two happy years flew by, and the Hansenide (leper) Colony, expanded toward its eventual capacity of 500 patients. Six days a week and often far into the night, the growing band of missionaries worked tirelessly for the physical and spiritual well-being of the people around them.

Only emergencies were attended to on Sabbaths. Anything else waited while staff and patients gathered in the open air to worship God. With Sabbath School picture rolls as his visual aids, Len told the people Bible stories and taught them the wonderful truth of a God who loves all mankind. He taught them songs, too, some English and some in pidgin.

Old or young, the people loved to sing. There was no piano or organ to guide them, but with wonderful natural harmony they sang: "Red and yellow, black and white, all are precious in His sight," or, "Shall we gather at the river?" or, "Lift up the trumpet and loud let it ring, Jesus is coming again." They might have had only the haziest idea of what a trumpet was, but what did it matter? The joy they received from singing to the true God was the important thing.

This was important because the native people in this Togoba area worshiped Kur. No one had ever seen Kur, but the chief of each village kept a highly valued, carefully guarded, sacred stone that symbolized Kur's presence.

Before engaging in intertribal battles, the village warriors prayed to Kur and offered oblations of pigs' blood to the sacred stone. If serious illness struck tribal members, they propitiated Kur with offerings of pig blood. Once a year each village held a sing-sing on a hilltop ceremonial ground. Here they danced all night to the wild beat of drums and sang and feasted and made offerings to their stone god.

Len hated these sing-sings. He hated the monotonous, dirgelike chantings. He hated the eerie sight of hundreds of half-naked, greased, brown bodies shining in the firelight as the dancers went round and round in a circle, clapping their hands and stamping their feet.

"It's all so devilish," he said to Mavis. "It depresses me. I wish we could make a greater spiritual impact on them."

"It's the squealing pigs I hate." Mavis shuddered. "I'm sure the poor creatures know that they're about to be bashed to death—"

"—And be roasted over a fire and eaten." Len finished for her.

"Mavis, we must build a church. These people respond so slowly to the love of God; it might help if we had a church, some holy place that they could *see*."

"It might," Mavis responded doubtfully, but Len was already on his way to look for suitable land.

There was not much available. The hill people depended on

their gardens for food, and land suitable for cultivation was precious. The government had experienced trouble enough getting the large area on which the leper colony stood, and Len could not expect to buy any more.

"We'll have to use some of the colony land," Len reported to the others.

"But that's all taken up with huts and houses and hospital gardens," the nurses pointed out. "There's scarcely a level inch left."

"There's still the site where our grass house burned down."

The women fell silent. Everyone knew why that plot had not been built on again. That piece of ground had once been a ceremonial sing-sing area, and the people persisted in regarding it as belonging to the devil-god, Kur. Many of them still insisted that the reason the missionaries' house burned down in the first place was that Kur didn't want them there.

"Yes, it's the only suitable place," the others reluctantly agreed with Len, " and it belongs to the government now. But will anyone help you erect a church there?"

"I'll find out."

Most of the local Togoba chiefs and their men refused to work on the site, but, eventually, a distant chief with an eye for business, agreed to accept the building contract. The locals looked on uneasily and muttered dire predictions as Len happily brought the mission's newly acquired tractor along to level the site.

The tractor was a great novelty. Few of the people had ever seen such a machine before, and they crowded around cheering and chattering, excitedly following Len as he drove toward the site.

One youth, showing off in front of his fellows, raced a little ahead and jumped onto the tractor's front axle. Len braked violently, but before the tractor could stop, the young fellow was thrown off. He fell in the tractor's path, one of the rear wheels rolling over his body, and one of the sharp, pronglike ends on the cultivator gashing his thigh.

Blood streamed from the wound, and the youth yelled in pain. The watching women wailed and tore at their hair in mourning, as if the lad were already dead. Eager hands rushed him to the clinic, and as Len sutured and dressed the ugly gash, he thanked God that no bones had been broken and no lasting injury done.

But the psychological damage was irreparable. The local people interpreted the accident as a direct indication of Kur's displeasure, and the building contractor and his men became noticeably nervous. They continued on the job only because they wanted the money. They muttered sullenly among themselves, and the building operations proceeded slowly.

Again and again Len tried to encourage the men to greater efforts by pointing out that his God was the Supreme Being, the God above all gods, and they had no need to fear the devil. But superstition is deeply ingrained, and the workmen regarded him sulkily and remained obviously unconvinced.

One day Len's work took him close to the church-building site. The men were trying to raise the heavy framework for the roof, so Len paused to watch. They had no modern tools and no machinery to help with the task. Rope and muscle provided their only power. With some men pushing, others pulling, and all of them shouting different orders, the heavy, bulky frame slowly tilted upright.

Then one of the ropes snapped. A prop slipped. And before anyone realized what was happening, the whole top-heavy structure crashed to the ground. In the first few seconds of shocked silence it seemed that no one had been hurt. Then Len saw a workman lying on the ground and raced across to him. One of the pushing poles had fallen on and crushed the young man's skull. No medical aid could save him.

As Len bent over the dying youth the wild-eyed workmen crowded around, shrieking their sorrow. To demonstrate the depths of their grief they scraped up handfuls of dirt and threw it into the air. They rubbed clay on their bodies and in their hair and shouted at the top of their voices, relaying the horrifying news to the primitive people in the nearby villages.

Men and boys from all around rushed to the site, screaming and beating their bare chests with anguish. Within minutes an angry, riotous crowd, more than a hundred strong, surrounded Len and the victim.

In the midst of all the confusion a sudden impulse made Len look up. Temba, one of the workers had crept around behind him and now stood with raised ax about to descend on Len's head.

"No!" Len shouted and wrestled the ax from him. Temba released his hold, but the look of hatred in his eyes told Len that he had not heard the last of the matter. Clearly Temba held Len responsible for the accident.

The mourners carried the young man's body off to his village, and Len trudged dejectedly back to his house. There'd be trouble now. The natives believed in the "payback" system and would not be happy until they killed someone to pay for the youth's death. Len sighed. As fast as the gospel made some headway, the devil erected a roadblock. Well, there was nothing he could do if the natives attacked them. No police or soldiers to call upon for help.

As he walked along, Len prayed for guidance as to how he should handle the situation. Len reached his house and mounted the steps, but before he opened the door, a slight sound made him swing around. Temba stood behind him with hate-filled eyes and a long fighting spear in his hand. Temba and two other spear-carrying men had silently followed him home.

"You killed him!" Temba shouted. "You build on Kur's ground. Kur no like it. Your fault."

"I did not kill him," Len answered quietly. "It was an accident. I am very sorry it happened, and we will pay his father a reasonable compensation; but I will discuss the matter with him, not with you. Put away those spears and go to your village."

Len entered the house and closed the door behind him. Inside, Mavis, the nurses, and five-year old Sharyn looked at him with fear-filled eyes. They had heard Temba's shouted accusations and guessed that something terrible had happened.

"Your fault. Kur no like." Wildly waving his spear, Temba rushed forward and pushed the door open. Len closed it and fastened the flimsy latch. Again Temba pushed it open, and again Len closed it.

Three times Temba pushed the door open and tried to enter the house. Spurred on by hate and the jibes of his supporters, he had lost all reason.

"Do not touch my door again," Len warned him. "Go back to your village, Temba."

Temba ignored the warning and tried to push past Len and intimidate the women. The situation was becoming desperate. Despite his determination not to use force, Len could think of nothing else to do. He shoved the hate-filled native to the edge of the veranda, and Temba fell down the steps.

The two friends laughed uproariously. Furious at losing face, Temba sneered up at Len, shook his spear threateningly, and stalked off.

"Thank You, God," Len breathed and turned once more toward the door. His hand shook as he fastened the latch.

"We were all praying, Daddy." Sharyn ran and flung her arms around her father. "We all prayed that the angry man would not hurt you."

"And God wonderfully answered your prayers, Darling." Over the child's head Len looked at Mavis and the nurses. They nodded. Each one knew that what could have turned into a terrible tragedy had been averted by prayer.

Eventually the whole sad business was sorted out and settled to the bereaved family's satisfaction, but for some time all work on the church was abandoned. Then Len heard of a Christian young man who would come and oversee the job.

Every morning before they began work, Yobik gathered the men around him and prayed for God's protection. He urged the laborers to take care and assured them that if they did their part God would do His.

With a God-fearing man in charge, the church soon took shape, and in a short time it was dedicated to the glory of God. Kur gradually lost his power in the minds of the highland people, and many turned to God with all their hearts. Instead of the mind-chilling, primitive dirges of the devil worshipers, the old sing-sing site rang with praises to the God of heaven and earth.

Chapter 7
Kai and Kur

Love for God and their suffering fellow men motivated the Barnards, the nurses, and the many other helpers who came and went at the leper colony. They worked long hours, and there was no such thing as "clocking in" and "clocking out" or union hours or days off. When there was work to be done, they did it.

But nothing made them happier than seeing the results of their work. Leprosy arrested and the sufferers sent back to their homes, bad cases treated—the healing work provided satisfaction enough. But their greatest joy came, not from seeing healed bodies, but changed hearts.

Everyone who came to the hospital for treatment was invited to attend morning and evening worship and Sabbath services, and very few failed to accept the invitation. Some attended out of sheer curiosity. Others attended because they liked the singing. Still others saw these meetings as an opportunity to learn pidgin English. But some came because their heathen hearts were touched by God's love. These were the ones who made the missionaries feel that all their sacrificial toil was worthwhile.

Among those who came to the leper colony for treatment was a man named Kai. Leprosy had crippled his hands, deformed his feet and left them partially paralyzed, and ulcers covered his scaly skin. Like most of the people in the surrounding villages, Kai wore only the usual bone and pigs' teeth ornaments around his neck and a bunch of leaves hanging from a twisted grass belt around his waist.

For awhile Kai appeared no different from any of the hundreds of lepers at the colony. Then the missionaries noticed how regularly Kai attended worship and meetings. He sat as close to the front as he could get and seemed to drink in every word. Changes took place in Kai's appearance too. The heathen ornaments disappeared. He kept his body clean. Instead of the usual suspicious scowls to which missionaries were accustomed, Kai smiled. He showed his interest in spiritual things by joining the baptismal class and after the required lengthy instruction, he was baptized.

By this time Kai had made himself a valued participant in all the colony activities. His help proved particularly useful as an interpreter in the church services, and when new patients arrived at the hospital, Kai's beaming face and reassuring words calmed many of their fears.

One day news drifted into the colony that two nearby chiefs were preparing for a sing-sing to honor their devil-god, Kur. Kai appeared quite upset when he heard of their plan. That particular week the Sabbath School lesson had been about God's giving the Ten Commandment law to Moses from Mount Sinai, and this had evidently greatly impressed Kai.

Kai sent a message to the two chiefs inviting them to visit the leper colony. When they came, he showed them around the wards and the gardens, and then took them into the church and pointed out the picture roll still hanging from the rostrum rail. The artist had vividly portrayed the flaming majesty of God giving the law to Moses on the mountain. Pointing to this graphic picture, Kai told the chiefs about the true God who had created the world and given laws to govern the people who lived in it.

"Big fella Papa on top," Kai introduced God by His pidgin name and told the chiefs that God wanted everyone to be happy and live at peace. God wanted them to obey the laws which He had given for all mankind. One of those laws told people to worship Him, the Creator, not the stones that He had created.

Kai preached so eloquently and earnestly that he impressed

these heathen chiefs, and they agreed to stop worshiping Kur and to cancel plans for the sing-sing.

When Len heard of their resolve he shook his head gravely. "Tell them," he instructed Kai, "that this is a good thing that they have decided, but not all their people may like it. Tell them that we will come to their village next Sabbath afternoon and bring the picture roll. We will let their people see the picture for themselves, and we will tell them the story."

This arrangement delighted the chiefs, and they happily returned to their villages.

"These chiefs have a lot of power, but it won't be as easy as they think," Len prophesied as he told Mavis about the chiefs' visit. "We must pray that God will prepare the way for us."

Next Sabbath afternoon, Len and Kai and several other Christians hiked out to the head chief's village. Although it was quite close ("as the crow flies") it was a long way by foot, and they had to wade through streams and follow treacherous mountain trails over high ridges and through deep gullies. As they neared the meeting place, they sang loudly to alert the people of their coming, " 'E got place where 'e good fella more," the pidgin English version of "There's A Land That Is Fairer Than Day."

Presently, through the trees they saw the village huts and the chief and his men sitting cross-legged on the ground waiting for them. As soon as they stepped into the clearing, Len sensed the tension in the atmosphere. The chief received the visitors with the customary greetings but with a noticeable lack of warmth.

Behind the chief and his friends stood three men. They looked angry and had smeared their bodies with mud as a sign of their displeasure at the visit of the mission party. These men stared at Len, and the hostility in their gaze seemed to dare him to come any closer.

Behind these men rose the tall barricade surrounding their sacred area, the place where the holy Kur stones were kept. Across the pathway leading to the barricade Len noticed that several long twigs had been pushed into the ground, a New Guinea–type warning to KEEP OUT—or else!

Conscious of this change in attitude, Len decided to first gain their confidence. "We have not come to take away your sacred stones," he assured the gathering. "We have come to tell you about the true God who loves you. He is greater than Kur. Greater than any other god. If you wish to serve Him you will want to discard your devil worship and sacred stones, but we will not force you to make that decision."

No one replied to Len's words, so he stepped back and let Kai take over. Kai unrolled the picture and held it up for all to see. With his disfigured hands he pointed to the flaming fire, and in graphic pidgin he repeated the story of "big fella Papa on top" that he had told to the chiefs.

As interest in Kai's story grew, the tension eased. The chief appeared happier, and even the burly fellows in the background relaxed and listened with open mouths to Kai's stories.

As he watched the people's reaction, Len prayed silently that they would put away their Kur stones and decide to follow the Lord God.

Kai talked for several hours, assuring the villagers that God loved them and wanted them to love Him. The people sat spellbound, and when Kai ended his speech the chief arose and, addressing Len, asked whether the mission could send them a teacher to instruct them in God's ways.

Len's heart leaped for joy. His prayer was answered and another heathen stronghold opened to the Word of God. But he scarcely had time to offer silent prayers of thanks before the chief turned and beckoned Kai and Len to follow him.

With complete disregard for the warning twigs stuck in the ground, the chief led Kai and Len into the barricaded enclosure. Len had a few misgivings about following him in there. It could so easily be a trap. But they were doing God's business, and their lives were in God's hands. He would surely protect them.

As they followed the chief, Len noticed that the huts inside the enclosure had recently been renovated and decorated for the proposed sing-sing. Beside the doorway of the first hut, a highly ornamented grotto guarded the sacred stones. The chief reached into its dark mossy interior and drew out his Kur stone. Then the clan leaders, all except one, stepped forward and brought out their precious stones.

While Len waited in suspense for what might happen next, the chief led the party back to the meeting ground. There, one by one, each clan leader made a short speech and, with great feeling and drama, presented his stone to Len. When the ceremony ended, Len had fifteen stones to take back to the mission as evidence of the villagers' sincerity.

A week later a visiting missionary accompanied Len and Kai as once more they tramped rough trails to take the gospel to the second of the two chiefs. This meeting followed an almost identical pattern—the clans handed over their Kur stones and requested that the mission send them a teacher.

Len passed on their request, and the mission board acted quickly. Within a week a native evangelist from another district arrived in Togoba ready to begin preaching. Len provided him with a local man as an interpreter, and the two started off for the first village.

After hours of walking, they were nearing the huddle of huts when a group of frowning, unfriendly men accosted them and asked who they were. The interpreter explained that his companion was a teacher, and the chief had asked for a teacher to come to his village.

"No, we don't want a teacher," the men shouted. "Go away. If you come to our village we will kill you."

The missionaries tried to argue, but the more they argued the more angry and aggressive the men became. One of them picked up a thick stick and rushed at the two Christians, savagely beating them about the head. "If you don't go, I'll kill you now," he shouted as he brandished the weapon. "Go! Go!"

At that very instant a passing cloud poured out a deluge of rain that made the murderous villagers run for cover. Taking advantage of the storm, the two missionaries fled back the way they had come. A friendly native at the foot of the mountain allowed them to shelter in an empty hut until the rain stopped. Then, crestfallen and discouraged, they trudged the long miles back to the colony and reported their failure.

"Never mind," Len cheered them. "We'll just wait awhile

and see what happens. This is God's work, and we are doing His will. If He wants you in that village He will work it out."

A week passed and nothing changed. Then, as night fell on the eighth day an excited group of men staggered into the colony carrying a crude stretcher on which lay a little girl. While playing with other children, nine-year-old Piam had fallen off a high rock and broken her arm. The bone above her elbow protruded through the flesh, and she screamed in agony if any movement jarred her.

Quickly the nurses prepared instruments and anesthetized the little girl. Len carried her into the operating room and began to set the broken bone and repair the damage. Suddenly there was a commotion outside. The door burst open, and a man rushed shouting into the room, scattering the nurses and sending the sterilized instruments flying.

Demented with grief, the child's father had chopped off the end of one of his fingers and smeared his body with mud and blood. When he saw his daughter lying unconscious on the operating table, he obviously thought that she was dead. Shrieking his sorrow, he pushed Len aside and grabbed her up, holding the little body to his chest and wailing unintelligible words.

Len and the nurses tried to explain, but they could not speak the father's language. They called for help, and some of the local natives ran in and managed to soothe the griefstricken man and maneuver him outside so that the operation could proceed.

When it was all over and the little girl's bone was set, the nurses carried her into a ward. Soon she recovered consciousness, and when her father realized that she was not dead, he calmed down. Through an interpreter Len explained to him that in about six weeks the child's arm would be as well as ever.

The man seemed to understand. He settled down quietly beside his daughter's bed and caused no further trouble.

Next morning as Len did hospital rounds and visited his newest patient, he noticed that the interpreter who accompanied him stared long and hard at Piam's father.

"What's the matter?" Len asked him as they walked across

to the next ward. "Do you know that man?"

"Yes." The interpreter's eyes widened. "This fella man tasol make 'im big fella trouble time me fella visit 'im village bilong 'im [This is the very man who beat us and threatened to kill us when we tried to enter his village]."

"Is that so?" Len thought a moment and then he said, "Well, don't let him know that you recognized him. We will just wait and see what happens while he's here."

Experience had taught Len to keep patients at the hospital for the duration of their treatment. If he allowed them to return home to their village half-cured, ignorant family or friends or the witch-doctors were likely to undo all the work he had done. For this reason he insisted that little Piam remain at the hospital for the full six weeks. Her father also remained to look after her.

The pair obviously found everything new and strange, but they entered into all the colony activities, timidly at first and then more boldly. They attended morning and evening worship and Sabbath services and listened with rapt attention to the gospel story.

By the time Piam's arm had healed, her father was eager to get home and tell his friends about the "big fella Papa on top." And when the preacher and interpreter visited the village again, there was no opposition to their coming.

Kai rejoiced at the seed sown in those villages, but he wanted to do more. One day he approached Len and asked for a picture roll. He said that he wanted to go to his own village and tell his family and friends about God's love.

"But, Kai," Len protested, "that is more than fourteen miles away. You could not walk so far." Len knew Kai's village. It sat on a low rise in the center of a filthy, mosquito-infested swamp. To reach it one had to wade knee-deep through mud and water for at least two hours. For anyone with deformed, half-paralyzed feet like Kai's, the journey would be a nightmare.

"I can do it," Kai insisted.

Len tried another tactic. "But, Kai, you need to stay here at the colony. Your treatment isn't nearly finished yet. If you left now the leprosy might flare up again, and then you'd be worse off. God would not expect you to risk your health when you can work for Him just as well right here."

But Kai was not convinced. "Leg bilong me no good, hand bilong me no good, skin bilong me no good, tasol neck bilong me good fella," he argued in pidgin.

Len fell silent. Kai was insisting that even though his feet, hands, and skin were effected with leprosy, there was nothing wrong with his voice.

"All right," Len gave in. "Come around tomorrow, and I'll give you some medicine and bandages to take with you. I have a spare pair of sandals too. I think they will fit your feet."

The next morning they prayed together, and Len watched with mixed feelings as Kai set out with the precious picture roll tucked under his arm and his few possessions tied in a bundle on his head.

A few weeks later, Len sent another man to Kai's village to help with the teaching and preaching, and in a short time the two men sent a message back that they had erected a church and wanted Len and the mission president to come and dedicate it.

People from villages far and near attended the dedication ceremony, and, at the conclusion, eight leaders of local clans rose and with great dignity surrendered their Kur stones. They told Len and the president that they now believed in the true God and wanted to follow Him.

Kai's face beamed with joy when he heard the men's speeches and saw them hand over their devil-stones, but Len saw lines of pain there also.

"Is something wrong?" he asked as soon as he could get his former patient alone.

Only then did Kai confess that he had worked so hard during the erection of the church that one of his feet suffered injury. A toe had turned gangrenous, and he felt sure it would have to come off.

"All right, come back to the hospital with us tomorrow, and we'll amputate it for you."

But Kai would not listen to that proposition. He could not

possibly leave his flourishing missionary work.

"Can't you cut it off here?" he pleaded. "It's only a no-good toe. Can't you cut it off while you're here?"

In vain Len pointed out the dangers of such a suggestion. He emphasized the lack of equipment and risk of infection. But for each of his arguments for going to the hospital, Kai had a better one against.

"If I go back with you, that means I have to walk fourteen miles there and fourteen miles back again," he pointed out. "That will make my foot much worse than it is now. Please cut it off here."

Kai's pleading was so effective that once again Len gave in. On a hastily erected operating table made of poles and branches, with an audience of half-naked natives watching his every movement, Len injected morphine into Kai's foot and removed the infected toe.

When Len revisited the village about three months later, he found that by a miracle of God, Kai's wound had healed perfectly. Not only that, but in the same period Kai and his helper had raised up a church of one hundred and ten worshipers and had thirty-two attending a baptismal class.

"Praise God for such workers as Kai," Len wrote to the mission president. "He walks where others fear to tread."

Chapter 8
Footslogging in the Mountains

Months stretched into years, and the reputation of the leper colony continued to spread. Lepers came from farther and farther away, and the resident community grew to nearly 500 patients. During the same time, the type of medication given also improved. When Len first cared for lepers, the only proven treatment consisted of a lengthy series of painful injections. Now the disease could be arrested by medicine administered orally.

But while many lepers came in for treatment, almost as many others didn't. Laila was one of them.

Laila lived in a heathen village far from the leper colony. In young manhood Laila was unaware that he had the disease, but as he grew older, the telltale symptoms became more pronounced—thickened ear lobes, white patches on his brown skin, loss of feeling in affected parts.

For a long time Laila managed to hide his condition and live a nearly normal life. But the leprosy gradually grew worse, and the villagers noticed it and banished him from their midst. Ignorant as they were, these primitive people knew that leprosy could be spread by contact. Even then Laila managed fairly well. He built himself a grass hut near a water supply and dug a garden. With the occasional bird or small animal that he shot with his bow and arrows, he managed to provide himself with food.

But as the disease devoured his body, Laila grew increasingly sick and weak. Finally, he could no longer work his small garden or hunt birds with his bow and arrows or cut firewood to cook his food. He became entirely helpless.

Every few days some of Laila's family or friends brought him just enough food and firewood to keep him alive. But sometimes they didn't have enough for themselves, or they were away fighting a tribal war and forgot about Laila.

Poor Laila. He knew nothing about the hospital and the kind treatment he would receive there. Even if he had known, there was no way he could make such a long journey. He just lay in his filthy, miserable hut, hungry, helpless, and hopeless.

One day half a dozen stalwart young men came to visit Laila. "There is going to be a big sing-sing feast," they told him, "and we want you to come."

"I can't walk," Laila said weakly. "I am too weak to attend any celebration."

"We'll carry you," the men offered. Hurriedly they cut poles and vines and made a crude stretcher. They helped Laila onto it and then set off through the jungle. All the while they talked pleasantly to him, telling him all the village news and describing the roasting pigs and the huge amounts of food the women were preparing for the feast.

Laila's eyes shone with anticipation. He had not eaten food like that in years. Thoughts of the coming feast so excited him that he did not notice how far into the jungle they had walked.

The men crossed a stream and started along the bank on the other side, and then Laila looked around. This was unfamiliar territory.

"Where are you going?" he asked. "This is not the way to the sing-sing ground."

"Oh, this is to another place," the men assured him. "It's only a little farther now."

Another dozen paces and the men halted beside a big hole that had been dug in the soft soil. "Now," grunted the leader, and the men carrying Laila suddenly tipped the crude stretcher. The sick man slid off into the hole, and the rain of earth and stones filling in behind him forever silenced his screams.

"That's dreadful!" Len exclaimed when the story of Laila's

fate reached his ears. "If only we owned a plane, that tragedy need never have happened." Len paced back and forth across the living-room floor while Mavis and Sharyn and little Kaye looked sympathetically on. (By this time the Barnards had added another member to their family.)

"If people can't come to us for help, we've got to go to them," he said at last. "We've got to visit these heathen villages and let them know we're here."

Mavis nodded. She understood how Len felt, but after all the problems they'd had at the beginning, everything was going well at the colony now, and she was happy to enjoy a respite from worry.

In fact, everything was going so well that Len had become restless. He could not forget his dream of flying, and whenever mission or General Conference officials visited the colony, he told them that he wanted to get out into the villages and begin new work.

"Anyone can do what I am doing here," he would explain. "I have trained dozens of 'dresser boys' to treat the less-serious cases, and with a doctor in charge, and maybe an extra nurse to help Elsie and Olive, the colony can easily get on without me. I want to go out into the villages and treat the sick and carry the gospel message where white men have never been."

Len would then lead the visiting official out onto the veranda and point to the treeclad mountaintops, stretching like dark green waves to the cloudflecked horizon. "There are hundreds of villages out there. Villages where the gospel has not penetrated, where people are still head-hunting cannibals."

"But, Len, those villages are almost inaccessible. You'd have to walk for weeks to get to even the nearest of them."

"Ah," Len said knowingly and prepared to deliver his punch line, "we could use airplanes." Then before the official recovered enough to protest, Len rushed on. "We could clear small airstrips at various strategic centers, establish a school and a clinic, and branch out from there to work the villages. It would be like spokes from the hub of a wheel and we—"

"Too costly," the mission officials would invariably reply, brushing Len's idea aside.

Undaunted, Len explained the cost per hour of flying to distant places compared with the cost of hiring carriers and tramping along jungle trails to reach those same places while risking death and disease from a dozen different sources.

"So you see," Len would crow triumphantly, "it saves much valuable time as well as money. A village that takes days to reach on foot can be reached in an hour or two by plane."

When they could not refute that argument, the officials would think of another objection.

"It'd be too dangerous," they said.

"Too dangerous!" Len exploded. "No one said it was too dangerous when thousands of us servicemen were sent to Papua New Guinea to risk our lives for king and country. How can it be too dangerous to do God's work in the same mountains and plains and with His blessing?"

"Oh well, perhaps someday." They all knew Len Barnard and his dreams of flying. Years ago Seventh-day Adventists had begun their work in Papua New Guinea with mission boats for the waterways and leather boots for the land routes, and this is the way they would continue. Slow perhaps, but sure.

Len's desire to become a front-line missionary began to take shape in 1955, when he handed the leper colony over to Dr. Roy Yeatts and he and Mavis were transferred to an established hospital and school at Omaura on the eastern extremity of the highlands.

From this outpost, Len and his native helpers branched out, carrying the gospel story to villagers who worshiped devils and lived in constant fear of death from disease or tribal fighting.

On one typical "walkabout," Len and his interpreter set off with a group of hired carriers. They would find no shops or motels in the jungle, so everything needed for the journey must be carried with them. Food, sometimes drinking water (or at least a kettle to boil it in), folding beds and plenty of blankets for the chilly nights, lamps and matches, changes of clothing, picture rolls, medicine chest, and gifts for the village chiefs—all had to be carried.

Assembling everything and arranging the head load for

each carrier was a task in itself. Mavis took care of the food and clothing department and checked the items off her list. Len and his medical assistant packed the medical requirements, and everyone else gave advice. If the party reached their first camping place and found that they had forgotten to include something—they just had to do without it.

All went well for the first few miles. The carriers sang as they tramped along. Then the trail grew steeper, and they saved their breath for the climb.

They forded shallow streams and edged perilously across deep chasms using fallen trees or knotted-vine bridges. Thick mud clung to boots and bare feet alike, and the men slipped and slithered up the steep hillsides. It seemed to Len that for every two steps forward they slid one step back.

Trekking like this hour after hour and day after day made Len's leg muscles ache. Every fiber of his being rebelled at the unnecessary torture. "If we had a plane," the thought tormented him, "if we had a plane we needn't climb these wretched mountains. We could fly right over them."

Toward the end of their third day's march, the party halted at a deep ravine. A fallen tree had once bridged the dangerous gap, but scars on the weathered trunk showed where it had been deliberately chopped apart and rendered useless.

"Two fella village 'e fight too much." Coming up behind Len, the foremost carrier pointed to the ax marks and Len sighed. Apparently two villages had fought, and one lot had cut off the others' retreat by ruining the bridge.

Now what would the mission party do? They could not go forward, and they had come too far to go back. Len squinted at the setting sun. A quick look around revealed another nearby tree that appeared long enough and strong enough to bridge the ravine. "Let's try it, boys," Len said with determination. Shouting encouragement to each other, the carriers downed their bundles and grabbed their large bush knives. In a short time they had chopped through the trunk, and with a mighty crash, a second tree fell across the gap.

Now that it was felled, the slender trunk looked anything but safe, and no one wanted to be first to cross. Len peered over the edge of the ravine. It was a long way down to the rocky bottom, and death or serious injury awaited anyone whose foot slipped. Calling the party around him, Len prayed aloud for God's protecting hand to cover them all. Then, like a good leader, he gingerly edged his way across, and the ladened porters followed.

Daylight still lingered as the last man safely reached the opposite bank. The party paused to give thanks to God and then hurried the remaining few miles to the village.

The villagers welcomed them warily. At Len's request they provided a sleeping hut and firewood and then gathered around to hear what the missionary had to say. Through his interpreter Len told them that he had come to treat the sick and tell them some good news. But he and his men had walked a long way, and they were tired. Tomorrow they would talk.

The next day Len opened the medicine chest and began treating the sick who lined up for his attention. He extracted aching teeth and cleaned and bandaged festering sores and huge tropical ulcers. He lanced boils and gave injections for yaws and other tropical ailments. Nearly everyone in the village seemed to have some sickness, and Len worked all morning seeing patients.

In the afternoon he called the people together. They all sat on the ground in the center of the village while he brought out his picture rolls and told them stories of Jesus and His love for all mankind.

News spreads quickly by "bush telegraph," and a few hours later a group of men from another village crept stealthily out of the jungle. They wore ornaments of bones and dried berries and were naked except for belts of twisted grass around their waists. They carried fighting spears and bows and arrows, but despite their fierce appearance they glanced nervously about as they neared the circle of listening people.

Len pretended not to notice the savage-looking visitors and kept right on telling his stories. Gradually the newcomers relaxed. First they squatted on their haunches, ready for either a fight or a flight. Then, as they became more and more interested in what they were hearing, they sat down and laid their weapons on the ground beside them.

As the hours passed, the two groups of natives eyed each other with less hostility. They still kept a reasonable distance apart, but when the newcomers showed no aggression, the others made no attempt to drive them away.

Eventually Len finished his picture-roll stories, and the chief of the host village arose. As spokesman for his tribe, he told Len that they were tired of living in fear of their lives.

"We are always at war with one tribe or another," he said. "We never know when our village will be raided and burned. Our women dare not go out to tend their gardens unless the men are there with weapons to protect them. We cannot visit our neighbors or they us. We lie in wait beside paths and kill one another.

"But now you have told us of a good way," the chief continued. "We want to live this way and be at peace. Won't you send someone to heal our sick and teach us a better way of life?"

Then the chief of the visiting tribe rose and addressed Len. He and his people were tired of warring too. They were tired of trying to appease gods who hated and punished them. They saw how clean and happy the mission boys looked. They wanted to be like that. Could they also have a teacher?

And so the work went on year in and year out. Mission workers pressed farther and farther into the wild hinterland of Papua New Guinea and unentered villages, either heathen or Christian, became less and less accessible. As a consequence, the long expeditions to visit them became more and more time consuming and costly.

Every three or four years the Barnard family returned to Australia for furlough, and Len was in great demand to tell stories at churches and camp meetings. He painted graphic word pictures of the mission field and told of miraculous escapes from danger. He spoke of healings and heart-gladdening conversions as village after village turned to God. But he never passed up an opportunity to point out how much faster the work would go if the Adventist Mission had a plane.

"Other denominations working in Papua New Guinea have airplanes," Len said passionately. "I see them flying overhead while we and our carriers are slogging up some torturous mountain trail. A couple of hours later, I see the plane return. They have gone right across the island and back again in the time it has taken for us to plod a dozen weary miles."

Len never asked for money. The union mission frowned upon such personal fund raising, and it was against church policy as well. But many times as the congregation filed out of a meeting, a generous member would press a check or some cash into Len's hand and whisper, "Put this toward your plane, Brother Barnard."

Not that the plane would be "his plane." Len made that clear to church officials. Time and again he told them, "If someone gives me a plane, I will hand it straight over to the mission. I don't want a plane for myself. I want it for God's work."

By the time his latest furlough ended, Len had collected a sizable amount of money toward the purchase of a plane. A namesake in America, Doctor James Barnard of Bakersfield, sent Len $500 to "start the ball rolling." Another American, Doctor Glen Reynolds, assured Len that he could get him a used plane at a reasonable price. A generous Australian church member donated $2,000, and others gave smaller amounts. With all this encouragement, Len felt reluctant to hand over his "airplane money" for general purpose use.

"What am I to do with this money?" Len took his problem to the union treasurer. "It was given to me specifically for a mission plane. It should not be used for other purposes. Shall I give it back to the donors?"

"Oh no, no. Don't give it back." The treasurer's spectacles trembled on his nose. "No, no, don't return the money, Brother Barnard. We'll think of something."

And they did. After years and years of opposition to his idea, the union committee finally voted that if Len received enough money to buy a plane, they would look with favor on his venture. When news of this action reached Len, he nearly went wild with excitement. His dream was on the way to becoming a reality.

Chapter 9
Wings Over New Guinea

Now that the union committee looked with favor on his project, Len redoubled his prayers and preparations. He fully expected that within a short time he would have received enough money to buy a plane. But God was not ready yet.

Having a pilot's license was one thing, but flying alone in sole charge of an airplane, was another. Len knew that he needed more experience, particularly in Papua New Guinea, and year by year he worked to add flying hours to his credit. Whenever the family went home on furlough, he hired a plane for practice. He sometimes got sympathetic pilots to let him take temporary charge of their planes and log more hours of flying time.

After the initial burst of enthusiasm for Len's dream waned, donations for the airplane slowed, and the next year added only another $1,000 to the fund. During the same length of time, several tragedies added to the urgency of the need and made Len all the more determined to fly.

Ruap and his wife, earnest, mission-trained young people, were appointed to work in a mountaintop village. To get there they had to plod many miles through the jungle and cross one 10,000-foot mountain pass so precipitous that the slightest misstep meant certain death on the rocks thousands of feet below.

The couple reached the primitive village safely and began working with the heathen people. Slowly their faithful witness to God's loving care for all of His children bore fruit, and in this once filthy and degraded village, a mission outpost gradually took shape. First Ruap erected a grass-roofed church to the glory of God and taught the people to sing praises and pray; then he and his wife began a small school in which to educate the bright-eyed youngsters. They taught the people how to avoid many diseases by practicing simple principles of hygiene.

Everything was going well until one day Ruap himself fell sick. His wife tried all the remedies that were available, but nothing helped. Ruap grew worse. He could not eat, and his legs felt weak and useless. Now Ruap became really alarmed. He realized that he must be suffering from some disease that was much worse than one of the usual jungle fevers. Ruap called for some of the village men and asked them to carry him to the nearest medical aid post.

But the villagers held a fatalistic view of disease and death, and they protested that it was not possible to carry anyone over such a dangerous trail. Not long rescued from blackest heathenism, they had not yet learned to have the faith and trust in God that Ruap had.

"Please," Ruap begged them, "please take me. I will pray to God, and He will protect and help you on the trail. If I don't get to medical aid I will die, and then who will tell you stories and teach your children?" While he pleaded with the people, Ruap and his wife also prayed that God would soften the men's hard hearts.

Finally the village headman gave orders, and a couple of the young men cut down long poles and laced them with vines to make a stretcher. They tied Ruap securely and, with his faithful wife trotting along behind, praying through her tears, the little group set off.

Down, down, down they went, slithering through mud, clambering over rocks, edging across terrifying chasms. Hour after hour they plodded on until at last they reached a government aid post.

The native orderly in charge did his best. He gave Ruap a series of injections which eased the pain but gave no lasting benefit.

"I can't do anything else," he told the bearers the next day. "You'd better take him to the mission."

Once more the group of carriers set off. Another two-day march before they arrived at the mission station where Len was in charge.

Len examined Ruap and then hurriedly sent a radio message: "Please send a plane," he urged the nearest government officer. "One of our workers is deathly sick. This is urgent. We must get him to a hospital immediately."

Word came back that the only available plane was not airworthy, but the men were working on it and would come as soon as possible.

For two days Len waited, doing everything he could to help the sick man, but Ruap's disease baffled him. The symptoms appeared much like the crippling poliomyelitis, yet different. Whatever it was, Len knew that he must not wait any longer. He must get his patient to the hospital fast.

With Mavis's help Len made a bed in the back of the mission Land Rover and drove the bumpy miles over largely dirt road to the mission hospital.

But it was too late. For eight agonizing days Ruap had tried to reach medical help. For eight days he and his carriers had suffered to make a journey that would have taken less than an hour by plane.

"If only he had gotten here sooner we could have saved his legs." The doctor shook his head. "Treatment can't help him now."

Ruap did not die, nor did he lose his faith in God. But he was crippled for life. Never again did he walk the mountain trails carrying God's message of salvation to isolated villagers.

Not long afterward, another near tragedy chilled Len's blood. Lamai and his wife traipsed along a narrow, muddy track on their way to the mission outpost where he was in charge. As was the custom, the wife carried their baby son on her back in a *biloom*—a woven bag suspended from a strap around her forehead.

As they climbed the leaf-strewn trail made slick from recent rain, the woman lost her footing and fell backward, striking the baby's back against a protruding root. His little spine was injured, and for weeks he suffered in the hospital, threatened with permanent paralysis.

The baby survived with no permanent damage, but this near tragedy provided one more argument to back up Len's constant pleading for a plane.

Suddenly, unexpectedly, money began pouring in. God set the wheels in motion, and in a few months, the mission plane bank account rose to $12,000!—enough to buy a good used airplane. Jubilantly Len made plans for the purchase, but before the arrangements were finalized their furlough came around again, and Len and Mavis and their two daughters flew home to Australia.

While there, Len met a former Longburn College friend who handed him a $4,000 donation.

"Thank you," Len wrung his friend's hand. "And thank God. Now we can purchase a brand new plane."

But nothing is ever as easy as it seems. Many weeks passed before the crated Cessna arrived from America and was assembled and painted in Australia. Finally, the waiting was over. On June 27, 1964, an excited Len Barnard attended the dedication ceremony of the *Andrew Stewart*, named after a veteran missionary to the South Seas.

As he listened to the speeches, Len held a praise service in his own heart. For eighteen years he had prayed and worked for this day. For eighteen years the need had tormented him, and for eighteen years he had held a largely unused pilot's license. Now his dream had come true.

For once his furlough seemed far too long. Len could scarcely wait to get back to New Guinea with the little plane. Before leaving, it had to be registered and have the identifying "VH-SDA" painted in huge letters on its wings.

As Len had long predicted, the little Cessna VH-SDA became the workhorse of the mission. In cases of accident or serious illness, urgent pleas for help were relayed by radio and the plane became a flying ambulance. The *Andrew Stewart* carried food and school supplies, it transported denominational VIP's visiting around the field, and it shifted native workers from one area to another in one swift exchange flight.

Airstrips were not numerous in New Guinea, and in many places the missionaries still had to trudge along winding jungle trails that led through mosquito- and crocodile-infested swamps or climb almost unscalable mountains in pursuit of their work.

But all that would change. From then on, whenever a village opened its heart to the gospel, as well as erecting a church and a school, the people would clear land suitable for a small airstrip. As the gospel advanced, so did the airplane.

The plane provided Len with plenty of exercises in faith also. In the misty mountain highlands, each flight was an adventure. Len soon lost count of the times that the Lord saved him and the plane from certain destruction.

Most of the airstrips he used were merely small clearings in the jungle, reasonably level and equipped with nothing more than a windsock. But clouds were the greatest hazard.

Rain fell almost daily over the whole of Papua New Guinea, and from the scorching lowlands, the vapor rose in clouds so white and thick that they looked like ice cream. But there was nothing sweet about these clouds. They closed in about the plane, billowing above and below and cutting off every inch of visibility. With all familiar landmarks blotted out, Len had to fly entirely by the cockpit instruments.

Conscious every moment that the slightest miscalculation spelled disaster, Len prayed as he tried to rise above the writhing clouds. Up, up, up. The altimeter showed 10,000 feet, 12,000 feet, 15,000 feet. There was a limit to what the little plane could do. He had no hope of flying over the mountain tips. He must go between them—a risky business in the best weather.

Often, Len's passengers sat behind him rigid with fear at the thought of the unpenetrable jungle below or the mighty rivers or the jagged rocks. If the plane crashed, they knew there was no chance of survival. But Len sat calm and quiet in the pilot's seat, his eyes roving from instrument panel to cloud-fogged window and his lips moving in constant silent prayer.

For two years Len flew the length and breadth of Papua New Guinea. Most times, it seemed that his flights assumed the nature of a contest: the VH-SDA with God's pilot at the controls, battling the enemy elements of fog, rain, and wind.

Then one glorious, cloudless day when all the world seemed filled with peace and beauty, and when he was taking off from a properly equipped government-controlled airstrip—it happened.

Len planned to start this flight early before the mists and clouds rolled in. Today he was leaving office work and mundane mission duties behind and setting off for two days of "flying visits" to outer mission stations. He had a full flying agenda ahead: taking supplies to isolated workers; transferring native teachers from one village school to another; delivering Sabbath School supplies. The project would take many hours, and Len's pulse quickened at the prospect of so much flying.

Len climbed into the plane and warmed the engine for a moment before taxiing across the runway to where his first passengers and cargo waited. He shut down the engine by pulling out the lean mixture control, waited till the motor stopped, and then turned off the ignition key.

Len climbed out of the plane, and while his passengers prepared to board, he filed his flight plan. Then he turned to double check the VH-SDA. He routinely tested the propeller spinner for looseness, checked the eighty-eight-inch blades for chips or cracks, and then tested the compression by reaching high, grasping the tip of the propeller, and pulling down. Yes, there was good compression in that cylinder, but there were five more to test. Once more Len raised his arm.

Suddenly, in one of those freak happenings that no one can anticipate, the engine fired and spun the propeller. The next thing Len knew, he was lying on the runway about ten feet from the plane with his left leg spurting blood.

"Help!" Len yelled and grabbed his thigh in an attempt to stop the bleeding. Mavis saw what had happened and ran screaming toward him. One of the passengers rushed to the control tower, and another dashed to the terminal for help. In a few moments the airport ambulance sped across the tarmac.

The ambulance crew applied a tourniquet to Len's thigh, lifted him into their vehicle, and raced the seven bumpy miles to the government hospital.

The airport authorities had telephoned ahead, and four doctors awaited Len's arrival. A quick examination revealed that Len's leg bone was shattered and the flesh gashed so deeply that only a small flap of skin connected his thigh to his lower leg.

"We'll have to amputate," the chief surgeon muttered to the three assisting doctors. "There's no way of saving that leg."

"Oh, please try." Despite the shock and pain, Len realized his desperate plight. "I'm a Christian missionary pilot," he told the doctors and pallid-faced nurse. "I know God will heal my leg if you will do your part. Please, please try. People everywhere will be praying for me."

The doctors looked from one to another, and Len read the hopelessness in their faces. "Please try to save my leg," he begged once more.

The nurse pricked his arm with an injection, and as he slipped into unconsciousness on the way to the operating room, Len heard the surgeon's quiet reply, "There is no chance. No chance at all."

In the operating room, the chief surgeon, who had formerly been a heart surgeon in Europe, and his colleagues set to work. They made a more detailed examination of Len's leg and decided to try to save it.

There was no blood bank in New Guinea and none of the most up-to-date surgical equipment, but one of the nurses gave her blood, and the doctors set to work with what they had.

Outside the operating room, the news had already spread across Papua New Guinea, and in mission stations of all denominations, people pleaded with God to save Len's leg and life. In Australia, shocked officials received word of the accident and knelt in prayer on his behalf.

One hour passed. Two hours. Mavis sat in the waiting room with Len's boots in her lap and tried to condition herself to the idea of a crippled husband. What could they do? Where would they go? No one would employ a one-legged missionary. What would Sharyn and Kaye say when they heard? The eternal minutes dragged by as she waited numbly for Len to be wheeled out of surgery.

At last the gurney appeared. Mavis leaped to her feet and followed it into a ward. Gentle hands lifted Len's limp form onto a high bed, and Mavis burst into relieved tears when she saw the plaster cast. They had not amputated after all.

"We'll try it for three days," the surgeon told her. "I don't hold out much hope, but we've done our best. If his leg becomes gangrenous, then we'll have to amputate."

"Thank you for trying," Mavis responded through her tears. "God can work a miracle."

She sat beside Len's bed, waiting for him to recover consciousness. He moaned a few times and stirred. Then he opened his eyes, and she saw the bedclothes move as he twisted his right foot around in the bed. Mavis guessed that he was trying to feel whether he still had two legs.

She slipped her hand under the covers, and her probing fingers touched the foot sticking out of the end of the cast—it was warm with circulating blood.

"It's still there, Len," she said, "and it's going to be all right."

"Thank You, God," Len said, and dropped off into peaceful sleep.

Chapter 10
Prayer and Persistence

The three days passed, and Len's injured leg showed no signs of gangrene. In fact, the healing process progressed so rapidly that in a short time he was allowed to leave the hospital on condition that he return to Australia and receive further treatment from an orthopedic specialist.

But Len's life of usefulness was over. At least that was the opinion of most people who heard about his accident. "You'll never be able to get around on that leg." His friends shook their heads sadly when they heard the full story and saw the unsightly scar above his left knee. "After an injury like that you'll be lucky if you can hobble."

But Len had no doubts. "Tell the boys I'll soon be back," he'd say cheerfully whenever missionaries on furlough called to see him before returning to their field. "Tell them I'm doing fine and to keep on working and praying."

The union committee failed to see any future for him either. Early retirement perhaps, or office work of some kind. Certainly he could not go back to piloting a plane or taking native workers on walkabouts. A pity, they agreed. Barnard was such a dedicated missionary.

But Len had no worries about his future. He prayed and he worked hard at helping God answer his prayers. Whatever treatment of exercise the specialist suggested, Len did it with all his might.

"I've got to get back to work," he said as he swung down the hospital corridors on his crutches. "And the sooner the better."

In a short time the specialist allowed Len to discard the crutches and try two walking canes. Then one.

At the end of eight months, the man who should have had his leg amputated was back at work in his beloved Papua New Guinea mission field.

One of the first things Len did when he reached Mount Hagen was go back to the government hospital and present himself to the chief surgeon.

"I can never thank you enough for the part you played in my recovery," Len said. "With the blessing of God I am able to walk around almost as well as ever: But one thing has bothered me. In my work at the leper colony I've amputated many leprous legs, and I know that the sciatic nerve and the femoral artery both lie well above that narrow flap of skin that held my upper and lower leg together. Can you explain how it was that my sciatic nerve and that important artery were not severed by the propeller blade?"

The doctor smiled. "I remember worrying about that as we worked on you, Mr. Barnard. But your bone was not cleanly cut. It was shattered. The X-rays showed a four-inch chip of bone that must have been pushed downward and protected the sciatic nerve. Your femoral artery was badly lacerated, but the chip also protected it from being completely severed."

"Oh God, how great Thou art," Len quoted, and the surgeon nodded.

In the years that followed, Len never tired of relating all the miraculous circumstances that attended his accident and recovery.

"If that propeller had hit me when I was out alone at an isolated airstrip, I'd have bled to death. The people out there are so primitive they wouldn't have known how to operate a radio-telephone if they had one. If it had happened when I was on one of my two- or three-day visits to distant workers, it would have taken many hours, if not days, to get help, and by that time it would have been too late to save my leg. I still don't know *why* it happened, but I know that God allowed it for some good reason."

As a result of his injuries Len could not make any more ten-

or twelve-day forays into the jungle with carriers and the picture roll. Younger missionaries took up that pioneering work. But he could still walk several miles over rough bush trails, and his injury did not interfere at all with his flying missions—or prevent him from working toward the fulfillment of another dream.

For years Len had talked of having native workers radiating out into unentered villages like spokes from a wheel hub.

"They'd operate from central mission outposts where there was an established church, school, clinic, and, of course, an airstrip. That would be the hub," he said. "The workers would not feel so isolated when they knew that they were only a few hours away from medical help in case of sickness or accident. They could get supplies more easily, too, and anything else they needed."

The president agreed that it was a fine idea, and soon after his return, Len began to put it into operation. To begin with he visited every mission station and outpost in his vast area. It thrilled him to see how well the native workers had kept things going during his long absence. Many of these men and their wives were only one generation removed from the most degrading heathenism, and yet they had shouldered responsibility and worked faithfully, without help or supervision.

Mavis did not share Len's love of flying. She was quite content to remain at the mission station and keep things going in his absence. But on one occasion Len persuaded her to accompany him on a visit to a village that had not long been opened to Christianity.

After a mere two-hour flight, Len brought the little Cessna down on an airstrip that had recently been hewn out of thick jungle. It was not paved in any way, not even smoothed over. "But at least they've removed the tree stumps and large stones." Len grinned as the plane jolted to a standstill and they emerged to stretch their cramped limbs.

They greeted the resident worker, inspected the reed-and-leaf church which he proudly showed them, and then Len had to take off again for an even more distant village.

"I'll do what I can here until you get back," Mavis promised, and started to open the boxes of medical and other supplies that they had brought for the worker. "I think I'll be plenty busy."

Several hours later Mavis looked at her watch. She could not expect Len back for some time yet. Well, that gave her plenty of time to make friends with some of the timid, semi-heathen women lurking in the background.

Looking about, Mavis spied a young woman sitting on the ground some distance away. She had a bundle in her lap that Mavis rightly guessed must be a baby. Ah, that made it easy.

Mavis quietly wandered in the direction of the woman, being careful not to hurry or alarm her in any way. Squatting down beside the mother, Mavis smiled and made signs that she would like to see the baby. She well knew that the quickest way to break down barriers is to admire a baby. Every mother, "red and yellow, black and white," is proud of her children.

Hesitantly the woman loosened the opening of the woven string *biloom* and disclosed a tiny baby wrapped below the waist in large green leaves. No more than two weeks old, the infant looked frail and dirty. But Mavis smiled and clucked admiringly and patted the baby's soft cheek. After a startled moment, the mother responded with a shy, proud smile.

As she continued to look at the little fellow, Mavis noticed something wrong with one of his hands. There were only three fingers on the tiny curled fist. Where the fourth finger should have been was only an ugly oozing sore.

How dreadful, she thought. Whatever could have happened? The baby's hand must be treated before infection set in and he became really ill. Mavis tried to explain to the mother that something should be done, but the woman only stared blankly. She did not understand Mavis's gesturing.

Mavis stood up. She'd have to go and find someone who could interpret for her. Where was the worker?

"Ask her what happened to the baby's hand." Mavis urged the interpreter when they returned. "How could such a tiny baby lose a finger?"

Obediently the interpreter asked a question, and the woman sullenly replied. He turned to Mavis.

"She bit it off."

"Bit it off? Bit off her own baby's finger? Why did she do that?"

There was some talk back and forth, and at length the interpreter explained. "This baby is actually her third child, but it is the only one living. The first two died when they were only a few months old."

Mavis nodded. She knew the high rate of infant mortality in the villages. Each year pneumonia, malaria, and dysentery killed hundreds of native children.

"But why did she do that?" Mavis indicated the tiny maimed hand.

"She's a heathen woman and believes that the devil is angry with her and killed her first two babies. She thought that if she bit off her baby's finger, it might placate the devil, and he would let this infant live."

Mavis sighed. "Tell her to let me treat the baby's hand, or he will die for sure."

As they walked back to the hut where she'd left the medical supplies, Mavis felt grateful that there was a worker here to teach these poor, ignorant people a better way.

In many places these native workers made the first contact with primitive tribesmen, teaching them the rudiments of the gospel and opening the way for white missionaries to follow and establish clinics, schools, and churches.

Although they physically resembled the people among whom they chose to live, these workers were no less courageous and no less missionaries than their white counterparts. For the gospel's sake they traveled far away from family and friends, and shared the privations and fears common to all isolated missionaries.

Pastor Piari was one of these noble men who managed the work in scores of heathen villages. A gentle-voiced, saintly man who stood bold as a lion against the forces of evil, he once entered a heathen village and found the whole populace gathered outside a hut where a little girl lay dying.

In answer to his questions, he learned that the child had been ill for several days and now had fallen into a deep coma and was scarcely breathing. Her death was imminent, and the women were already beating their breasts and chanting doleful dirges while the men were making surreptitious plans for a funeral feast.

"Let me see her." Pastor Piari edged his way among the mourners until he stood beside the child. The girl lay on a sleeping mat on the earth floor of her parents' hut. She looked so frail and still that Pastor Piari realized she was beyond any treatments that he could give.

His thoughts flew back to the Bible story of another little girl about the same age. When Jesus was on earth He had healed Jairus's daughter. If He could heal a child who was already dead, couldn't He heal this dying girl?

While the people around him continued to wail in heathen despair, Pastor Piari addressed the chief.

"Tell your people to be quiet and listen while I pray to the great God in heaven. He is greater than any devil or witch doctor. He can heal the sick and raise the dead to life."

More from surprise than belief, the people gradually ceased their wailing. They listened intently while Pastor Piari offered a simple, earnest prayer, asking God to give these people an example of His mighty power by healing the dying child.

The pastor had scarcely said "Amen" when the girl opened her eyes and looked around. A moment later she sat up.

"I'm hungry," she said in her native language.

While the women prepared food for the girl, Pastor Piari told the assembly more about God and His wonderful power to heal, not only sick bodies, but sin-sick souls.

With such evidence before their eyes, the people were eager to learn more and begged the pastor to stay and teach them. God had won a mighty victory over heathenism, and another village opened its arms to the gospel.

Chapter 11
Work for Your Dreams

When Europeans first began to live and work in Papua New Guinea, they found it almost impossible to avoid becoming involved in intertribal fighting. Missionary, policeman, gold miner, and government officer—all had tales to tell.

On one occasion Len met up with a government patrol officer who told him about some of his exciting escapes.

"A few years back," he said, "two tribes living high in the mountains fought so continuously that they wiped out whole families with their inter-feudal paybacks. In one instance, a man, his wife, and small son were all that remained of a once-thriving village."

" 'You'll have to go and stop it somehow,' the superior officer said. 'Be careful not to kill anyone, but arrest the ringleaders if necessary.'

"Yes sir." The young patrol officer did not relish such a dangerous task, but he assembled a group of native policemen, explained the situation, and outfitted them for a patrol.

"We must avoid trouble if we can," he told his men, "but if they will not listen—" He patted his holstered gun.

The patrol set out, and after days of arduous climbing into the mountains, they tried to make contact with the warring tribes. But the chiefs had their scouts posted along all the trails, and they guessed why the police were coming into their district.

Keeping the policemen in sight, the chief's men quietly crept through the jungle until they had the patrol at their mercy on a narrow ridge. From their high vantage point they sent a rain of arrows onto the unsuspecting patrol. Several of the native policemen fell, but the rest rallied, and at the officer's command they outflanked the tribesmen and sent them scurrying down the hillside. In their haste to escape, the frightened tribesmen dropped dozens of highly ornamented wooden shields and hundreds of arrows.

If the patrol leader hoped that their losses would discourage the warriors, he was disappointed. Instead of retreating to their villages, they prepared more arrows and hid in the jungle until night. When the campfires died down and the weary patrol officer and his men fell asleep, they crept closer.

Like silent shadows they slunk among the trees until they reached the shelter of some convenient boulders overlooking the camp. The single sentry on guard heard and saw nothing until the tribesmen suddenly shrieked their hate and showered the sleeping men with arrows.

The patrol officer awoke and leaped to his feet. Hand on his gun, he shone his flashlight in all directions, but his own men were milling around, and it was impossible to do anything constructive in the darkness. For the rest of the night the patrol took what cover it could, and at dawn the officer bravely approached the natural fortress and appealed to the hidden tribesmen to surrender.

They shouted defiantly at him and remained out of sight. He advanced toward their hiding place, spattering the rock with warning bullets as he came. Only then did the fighters capitulate, sulkily emerging from behind the boulders and laying down their spears and bows and arrows.

"You were lucky to get out of there alive," Len commented when the patrol officer finished his story.

"I sure was." The officer grinned. "But do you know what? Next time I visited that area, the people were like lambs. Formerly warring tribes now living in sweet harmony in adjoining villages. Almost unbelievable. You guys certainly know how to get results."

"Us?" Len sounded surprised. "What did we have to do with those fighters?"

Before the patrol officer could reply a sudden recollection stirred in Len's mind. "I know the people you're talking about. Cannibals, head-hunters, a terribly hostile crowd. As soon as the government declared the territory open—that must have been after your patrol—we sent a native worker in there. A few weeks later I visited him to see what progress he had made. The chiefs of the two main villages rather gingerly called their people together. But after we had talked for a while and told them some Bible stories, both chiefs stood up and said they had seen how clean and happy our mission worker was, and they wanted to be like him. They asked us to send them teachers because they were tired of warring and wanted to live at peace."

"They're the ones; that's Baira village." The patrol officer nodded. "You guys certainly know how to tame them."

"It's not us," Len said humbly. "It's the power of God working on their heathen hearts. We are only the tools in His hand."

As Len had anticipated during all those long years of waiting and praying, the *Andrew Stewart* played a vital role in soul winning.

One particularly stormy afternoon, when thunder reverberated around the mountains and vivid lightning pierced the thick, black clouds, Len received a message that two tribes were fighting in the nearby Porgera Valley area. A chief's head had been gashed with a stone ax, and he would most certainly die if help did not come quickly.

"It's not a good day for flying." Len squinted at the leaden sky. Earlier in the day two commercial flights had returned to base after unsuccessfully trying to battle the storm. Now it was late afternoon, and the storms were still venting their fury against the mighty mountains.

Cloud, wind, and tropical storms were Len's greatest enemies as he flew around ministering to the pockets of population nestled in folds between the mighty mountains. Poor visibility often hid jagged peaks that rose higher into the air than the little mission plane could ever hope to soar, and only his faith in God and his long acquaintance with the highlands helped him guide the plane between them.

Now, with his eyes still on the lowering clouds, Len shrugged. "I guess it's not the worst weather I've ever flown in," he told the local government officer who had brought the message. "With God's help we'll make it."

"We'll come with you." the officer, two native policemen, and a medical orderly joined Len at the airstrip. "I guess we'd better try and settle them down before any more damage is done."

The rain eased a little, and the cloud lifted enough for Len to see the end of the runway and take off. Before they had gone far, however, conditions deteriorated. Rain lashed the windows of the small plane, and wind buffeted its fragile wings. The passengers clung to the sides of their seats and avoided each others' eyes.

Finally, at 13,000 feet, a break in the clouds allowed Len a glimpse of the mountains below, and his earnest prayers were answered when he spied the tiny airstrip in Porgera Valley.

A few minutes later they landed safely and taxied to the end of the strip, scattering the warriors who had stopped fighting to mourn the dead and dying.

As fast as possible Len and the medical orderly loaded the injured chief into the plane and prepared for takeoff. Drifting clouds obscured the far end of the runway, but Len sped through it. Impending darkness and the seriousness of the chief's condition made immediate return necessary.

As the little plane fought its way upward and reached 10,000 feet, the chief lapsed into unconsciousness, and the watching orderly shouted, "Man 'e die finish."

Len groaned. Surely not. Surely he had not died. Not after all the risks they had taken to rescue him. Once more Len turned to God in prayer.

Night would soon be upon them, and Len's lonely mountain airbase had no lights of any kind. How would he find it if darkness beat them? Len prayed and pushed the little aircraft to its limit. But it seemed like hours before the little plane's headlights skimmed over the edge of the home airstrip.

A doctor in a waiting vehicle rushed the injured chief to the government hospital. A tomahawk had fractured the chief's skull, and brain tissue exuded from the gash, but expert treatment and a blood transfusion worked wonders, and the next morning he showed definite signs of improvement.

A few days later the chief sat up and talked rationally when Len visited him. Delighted at his recovery, Len told the chief how he had been rescued and pointed out how thankful he should be to the great God of heaven for saving his life and sending missionaries to Papua New Guinea to help him and his people.

Len lost count of all the times God saved him and the plane from destruction. Eighteen years of footslogging through swamp and jungle had taught him a healthy respect for the terrain. He well knew that one moment of carelessness could cost his life, and he never set out without praying for God's help and protection.

And so the weeks gave way to months and the months to years. Gray hairs peppered Mavis's auburn locks, and Len's hair thinned and finally almost disappeared.

The gallant *Andrew Stewart* aged also, and two new planes, donated by the "Quiet Hour" in America, took its place.

Pilots proliferated too, and by 1972, when Len and Mavis reluctantly said goodbye to their work in Papua New Guinea, there were eight fully trained pilots in the Seventh-day Adventist mission.

Looking back over twenty-five years in mission service, Len marvels at the way the Lord led him and what he has seen accomplished.

"Work for your dreams," he says to today's young people, "and never give up. It may take a little time for God to fit you for the task He has in mind, but it's worth the waiting."